DISCARDED

THE WILD TROUT

THE WILD TROUT

ROD SUTTERBY · MALCOLM GREENHALGH

WITH PHOTOGRAPHS BY

SIMON FARRELL

GEORGE
PHILIP
LONDON

British Library Cataloguing in Publication Data
Sutterby, Rod
The Wild Trout : the natural history of an endangered fish
1. Trout
I. Title   II Greenhalgh, Malcolm
597′.55

ISBN 0-540-01199-1

Artwork © Rod Sutterby 1989
Text © Malcolm Greenhalgh 1989

**First published by George Philip Ltd,
59 Grosvenor Street, London W1X 9DA**

Printed in Italy by L.E.G.O., Vicenza

'The wild life of today is not ours to dispose of as we please.
We have it in trust. We must account for it to those who
come after.'

His Majesty King George VI

FOREWORD

At 2.40 on the afternoon of Sunday, 17 July 1983, a violent thunderstorm broke over Kilhope Fell in the North Pennines. At three o'clock a wall of water, eight feet high, rushed down the valley of the West Allen Burn, sweeping away all in its path. By dawn the next day the flood had subsided, revealing such extensive damage that one geomorphologist suggested that a spate of this magnitude might occur only once in 4,000 years. The bed of the river had been rent asunder. Large areas of farmland had been eroded and replaced by jumbled heaps of huge boulders. Trees had been uprooted and swept off downstream. Five bridges were utterly destroyed.

The morning following the flood, Rod Sutterby's sons, Lee and Reuben, walked along the stream to look at the devastation. They returned to their home on the fellside an hour later, carrying a 56 lb fertilizer sack crammed with dead trout that they had collected from fields by the river. The sack was emptied on to the kitchen floor for Rod to observe the variety of form and colour of the fish. At first he tried to arrange the dead trout in one sequence, with the palest at one end and the darkest at the other. Soon he realised that this was not possible. Instead, the trout could be assigned to one of three categories: bright, silver-sided trout with blue backs and red spots; trout with orange flanks and green backs; very dark brown trout with huge heads and jaws.

This variation among trout from one small stream intrigued Rod, a professional artist who had for many years painted fish portraits as well as illustrations for angling books and magazines. Discovering the dearth of visual information on wild trout varieties, he decided to paint the portraits of as wide a range of trout, both European and American, as he could obtain. This was the seed from which *The Wild Trout* has grown. To accompany his series of paintings, Rod asked me to write a text which would highlight the need to protect wild trout from the hazards of our industrialized society. As a trained ecologist, and author of two books on fly-fishing, I shared Rod's fascination with the trout: indeed, I had given up full-time employment on my fortieth birthday so that I could research and write about my twin passions of natural history and angling. Rod also invited Simon Farrell, an old friend and a professional photographer, to provide pictures of wild trout habitats. The team was complete.

Artist, photographer and writer often work almost independently in the production of a book. *The Wild Trout* is special because the three of us have worked together. On a typical field trip, Rod might be found sitting outside his tent making careful drawings of a trout specimen, while Simon explored the nearby lake shore for a particular viewpoint, or watched the changing light, and I drifted in the boat, observing and fishing for trout. When the writing began, the telephone linked our homes in Northumberland, London and Cheshire; each member described his latest work in studio, darkroom or office, and sought advice or made suggestions to the other team members. In the later stages, as the book was finally brought together, Rod's house in Northumberland and the office of our publishers were the scenes of many long discussions. This book is the product: the result of three years' intensive work.

The Wild Trout is not an encyclopaedia of trout, nor is it a field guide for identifying all the trout varieties of the world. It is a record of our investigation of both Old and New World trout, a celebration of their different forms, a call to conserve this variation by protecting wild trout habitats. And by wild trout we mean trout that are born, grow, breed and die in their native waters; not trout that have been raised in fish-farms and

RIGHT
A gillaroo, one of Ireland's wild trout varieties, browses among the boulders of Lough Melvin.
Pastel and wash

6

released to the water, nor feral trout that have been introduced into regions of the world that formerly never held native trout.

The wild trout of Europe, Asia and North America need the cleanest of waters in rivers, lakes and the sea if they are to thrive. The trout's success is a measure of the health of our planet; for there is no better proof that our aquatic habitats are clean than their ability to support a thriving head of wild trout. We hope that in reading this book, anglers, naturalists, conservationists and others who may never have looked closely at wild trout will appreciate the beauty of these remarkable fish; and seeing the problems which man has imposed on the wild trout will join the growing movement in both Europe and North America to press for their careful conservation.

MALCOLM GREENHALGH
May 1989

Contents

ACKNOWLEDGEMENTS

This study would not have been possible without the assistance of many organisations and individuals. Limitations of space prevent us naming them all, but we wish to express our gratitude to the Water Authorities in England and Wales, the Departments of The Interior, Wildlife, and Fish and Game in the United States and Canada, correspondents in Europe and North America, riparian owners, providers of hospitality in the way of guides, boats, food and accommodation, and friends and families without whom this book would never have been produced.

THE PAINTINGS

'He is an intelligent kind of creature, and has evidently a will of his own—he looks sagacious and intelligent—preserves a superior and dignified demeanor unattainable by any other occupant of the streams. His physical condition is equally entitled to our respectful consideration. He boasts a prepossessing and fascinating figure, moulded in strict conformity with the most refined principles of symmetrical proportion, sparkles in all the gorgeous colours of the rainbow, and occupies a distinguished position in the important science of gastronomy.'

Robert Blakey, *Angling*, 1800

CHAPTER ONE

THE WILD TROUT

Almost 200 years have elapsed since the English naturalist Robert Blakey wrote his glowing description of the trout. Yet there can be little doubt that the term 'wild trout' still evokes feelings of high regard in the minds not only of naturalists, anglers and gastronomes, but of the great majority who have no special cause to think of fish in their daily lives. Possibly only the salmon, a close relation of the trout, is held in such high esteem. The sheer beauty of this powerful, fast-swimming, streamlined fish is a cause of wonder. Even the most apathetic observer will sit entranced by a stream when trout are taking flies from the surface, or by a waterfall when they are leaping upstream on their spawning runs. On countless occasions successful anglers have felt a glow of pride when passers-by have stopped to admire the catch: a big silver sea trout, a tiny speckled trout from a stream or a gleaming green-backed lake trout.

The variation among trout is fascinating to naturalists. Trout occur in a vast range of sizes and colours, and thrive in every continent except Antarctica. At least one species of trout can be found wherever there are streams or lakes capable of supporting a trout population; and neighbouring lakes or rivers may hold very different varieties. For thousands of years trout have been native to much of Europe, Asia and North America. In recent centuries, trout have been introduced to the parts of these regions where they did not formerly occur, and carried to the most distant corners of the world—to South America, eastern and southern Africa, Australia and New Zealand, and through the Far East as far as Japan.

For the professional ecologist and the conservationist, an added attraction of wild trout is the environment they live in. Trout can exist only in the cleanest of waters. The presence of a thriving population of trout in a river or lake, or a good run of sea trout through an estuary and inshore waters, testifies to the healthy state of that water. A corollary is that trout tend to inhabit waters that are set in the midst of beautiful, unspoilt countryside away from the despoliation wreaked by urban sprawl and industrialization. For naturalists, wild trout mean wild places.

Even city dwellers, living far from a trout stream or lake, have a special regard for the trout. Gourmets value its splendid appearance almost as much as its firm flesh, enriched with an oil that is high in vitamins. Until recently the trout was a very special fish, sold only in the most prestigious restaurants and by top-class fishmongers. Now trout are farmed so intensively that they are one of the least expensive fish on sale; but a fresh sea trout is still a great delicacy.

Of all the trout's admirers, however, none are more dedicated than the anglers who have raised trout fishing almost to an art form. Indeed the fascination of the trout has led many anglers to become naturalists and ecologists as well as fishermen; and the study and conservation of wild trout have gone hand in hand with the desire of anglers to catch them. At first sight this might seem an anomaly. However, trout anglers have been long aware that if their sport is to be good, they must look to water quality and the maintenance of trout stocks. And when anglers conserve a clean aquatic environment, they also help in the conservation of the other aquatic animals and plants that share the water with the trout.

Today trout and their habitats are under considerable threat from pollution and water abstraction, from over-fishing of sea trout by commercial net fisheries and from pressure on some inland waters by rod-and-line anglers. The introduction of other fish into a trout river or lake threatens the survival of some trout varieties. And the modern trend to re-stock lakes and rivers with farmed trout threatens the genetic integrity of some strains of wild trout. Not all trout are in danger; indeed, the population as a whole may even be growing in number. But recent scientific studies in the USA, Canada and the British Isles—some of which are still in progress—have suggested that some varieties of wild trout are in danger of extinction, unless measures are taken to protect them.

When birds or mammals or some of the rarer forms of wild orchids or butterflies are in danger, natural history enthusiasts campaign against these threats. But most amateur naturalists and natural history organisations pay scant regard to fish: after all, they are not easily watched or studied compared with land animals and plants. Their welfare is left to anglers and professional naturalists. However, there is a major problem in conserving the wild trout, because of the disparity of scientific opinion on the classification of trout varieties. At present, the dominant view is that most varieties are insignificant local variations of a single species. Where expert opinion does not recognise the wild trout of a particular lake or river as a unique variety, professional naturalists will not campaign to save it from extinction. Yet if the latest studies are a guide, future research may well prove current beliefs to be incorrect.

Today the care and conservation of the threatened varieties lies with the trout's admirers. One of the main reasons for producing this book is to bring this to the attention of naturalists, conservationists, anglers and the most general of readers: to all who love wild trout, wild rivers and wild lakes.

The angler's dedication to the wild trout can be traced back in history to the 3rd century AD, when the Roman writer Claudius Aelianus wrote in his famous work *De Animalium Natura*:

'I have heard of a Macedonian way of catching fish, and it is this. Between Beroea and Thessalonica runs a river called the Astraeus, and in it there are fish with speckled skins. These fish feed on a fly special to the country, which the natives call *hippurus*. These flies float on the water and when a fish observes a fly on the surface it quietly swims up, afraid to stir up the water lest it should scare away its prey. It approaches under its own shadow, opens its mouth gently and sucks down the fly, rather like a wolf carrying off a sheep from the fold or an eagle a goose from the farmyard. Having done this it sinks away below the ripple.

'Now though the fisherman knows of this, they do not use these flies at all for bait; for if a man's hand touch them their colour fades, their wings wither and the fish will not take them. They fasten red wool round a hook and tie on the wool two waxed-coloured feathers that grow under a cock's wattles. Their rod is six feet long, and the line is the same length. Then they throw their fly on to the water, and the fish, being attracted by the colour, becomes greatly excited, and comes straight at it, anticipating a succulent mouthful.'

If we accept that the 'fish with speckled skins' are brown trout, then this is the earliest known account of fly fishing: the first in a vast literature on that special relationship between trout, the fly-hunter, and man, the trout-hunter. Although Aelianus wrote in the 3rd century, some historians have considered that he plagiarised his account from an earlier 1st century AD text. If this is so, then the historical relationship between trout, fly and man is 2000 years old.

But it was in medieval England that trout fishing began to be transformed from a means of obtaining food to a field sport with its own rules and rituals. In 1496 Wynkyn de Worde, the successor to William Caxton at the Westminster printing press, published a second edition of *A Boke of St Albans* in which he included a supplement called *Treetyse of Fysshynnge wyth an Angle*. This was the first real attempt to describe in print the art of angling. Here was explained how to make fishing hooks from needles, how to make lines and rods. And, especially important, how to make the best twelve artificial flies for trout fishing, and how and when to use them. Through the next three centuries several texts on angling were produced and each of them duplicated, often word for word, the methods and the twelve trout flies of the *Treetyse*.

Even that most famous of writers, Izaak Walton, author of *The Compleat Angler* (1653) cribbed his trout flies from the *Treetyse*: 'You are to note, that there are twelve kinds of artificially made flies to angle with on top of the water. The first is the dun-fly, in March: the body is made from dun wool; the wings, of partridge's feathers. The second is another dun-fly: the body of black wool; and the wings made of the black drake's feathers, and of the feathers under his tail.' And so on, almost verbatim from the *Treetyse*.

English writers of the 17th and 18th centuries increasingly separated the trout from the other fish of river and lake. The reputation of the trout as the angler's worthy adversary, and its rich but delicate flavour on the table, raised its value above all others. The special relationship between the sports fisherman and the wild trout was rapidly developing; and in the 19th century a revolution in technique elevated trout fishing to a new status, worthy of the most sporting of Victorian gentlemen. On 5 June 1865 James Ogden, a professional fly-dresser from

Derbyshire in the English Midlands, took some artificial mayflies on to the River Wye where it was standard practice to fish for trout with the natural mayfly as bait. The fishery owner was so impressed with Ogden's imitative flies and their success that he outlawed the use of live bait and insisted that henceforth only artificial fly would be permitted. So furious were the other Wye anglers that they forced Ogden and his family to leave town. Later, the use of any method other than artificial fly was outlawed from many other famous English trout streams.

When it was founded in 1822, the Houghton Club, the oldest angling club in the world, permitted the use of natural baits on the River Test in Hampshire: fifty years later it was artificial fly only. The 'fly only' rule slowly spread and is still spreading to trout fisheries all over the world. Though some fisheries allow both fly and bait there is no doubt that a trout caught on fly is considered more worthy than one caught on bait. This is certainly not because trout are more difficult to catch with artificial fly, as many bait anglers imagine. In fact, the opposite is true. As Ogden showed with his artificial mayflies on the Wye, fly will beat bait on most days. The reality was that artificial flies were adopted as part of the regalia of 'game fishing' at a time when the owners of trout waters decided to conserve their fish stocks by reducing the number of anglers.

Through the 19th century the population of lowland Britain had increased so rapidly that the supply of trout was outstripped by demand. There was not enough trout fishing within easy reach of the growing towns and cities to allow everyone to participate. The wealthier upper and middle classes took over the trout waters and preserved them for their own use and left the coarse angling to the less well-off. This process was most marked on the chalkstreams of southern and central England, but even in northern England—where there is

relatively more trout stream—much of the fishing was jealously preserved. In Yorkshire, the Aire Fishing Club had no difficulty in demanding an annual subscription in 1894 of £6 6s from its 50 gentlemen members. Such a sum, which was by no means unusual, would have amounted to several weeks' wages for a mill-hand or farm labourer.

For the wealthy angler, fishing was not simply a matter of catching trout. New rules imposed what was considered to be a 'sporting' attitude to angling, and enforced gentlemanly good conduct. The first rule in trout fishing had been 'fly only'. With the invention of the dry fly, that floats high on the water and precisely imitates a natural insect, some clubs went as far as 'dry fly only'.

The attitudes of the Victorian gentlemen anglers spread throughout the world during the following decades. When middle-class entrepreneurs and army officers left Britain to settle in North America, Australia and New Zealand, East and South Africa and parts of the Far East and South America, they took trout fishing with them. If there were no trout where they went, then they introduced the fish, just as they did red deer, pheasants and rabbits for shooting. When they discovered new species of trout, they sent some back home. In North America where the rainbow trout is native, the European brown trout was introduced. In Europe, where the brown trout is native, there is now angling for rainbow trout and brook trout (properly called speckled char) from North America. And in many countries which had no native trout there are now rainbow trout or brown trout, or even both.

The rules of fishing travelled with the fishermen, regardless of local conditions. The English settlers who arrived in the United States and Canada in the late 19th century found an abundance of trout fishing, yet many chose to fish for these

trout with fly. As a result, the trout has become a very special fish throughout the world, revered by literally millions of anglers. And trout fishing is the subject of a literature more extensive than that of any other sport, including soccer, cricket and baseball.

'If our work will let us escape on Friday evening, it is a luxury; but even if we belong only to those in the middle state of happiness, who work till midnight or later on Friday, and can have the whole of Saturday and Sunday in the country, we may still be splendidly off, provided that we are careful to miss nothing. . . . The earliest trains leave Waterloo, the usual place for departure for the Itchen or Test, either at or just before six o'clock in the morning. At some time between eight and nine o'clock, you step out of the train, and are in a few minutes among all the long-desired things. Every sense is alert and every scent and everything seen or heard is noted with delight.'

Thus in his book *Fly-Fishing* (1899) wrote Viscount Edward Grey of Falloden, who complemented his work as a leading statesman in London's Whitehall with an inquisitive approach to angling and ornithology. Such men were the founding fathers both of trout fly fishing and modern natural history. They spent their week busy in the office and then, at weekends and during long holidays that the working classes could ill afford, they left town for the country where they exercised their minds with binoculars, microscopes, specimen jars, butterfly nets, fly fishing and fly dressing.

Today it is tempting to deride their Victorian attitudes and principles. But the enthusiasm with which they approached their pastimes and the effort they crammed into every spare

A steelhead (the sea-going form of rainbow trout) pursuing its prey amongst kelp off the Alaskan coast.

Pastel and wash

moment renders the modern naturalist and trout angler in their debt. It was men like Grey who were fascinated enough by the minutiae of their chosen sport to examine the trout in its habitat, observing its behaviour and life history, and questioning the reasons for the variation of size, form and coloration among the trout of different rivers and lakes.

Before the 19th century, trout were seen simply as a source of food and sport. Very few anglers or naturalists ever saw the varieties of trout that lived in lakes or rivers at any distance from their homes. Travel was both difficult and expensive, even in the British Isles, so to make a special expedition to catch trout more than a few miles away was out of the question. Consequently, the early descriptions of trout were very parochial.

Furthermore, until Linnaeus devised his system of naming plants and animals scientifically, the names given to the different forms of trout were based on regional colloquial preference. The Irish had their white trout, gillaroo, sonaghen and dollaghan; did it matter that these were incomprehensible to the English and Scots? The Welsh referred to the Atlantic sea trout as the sewin (and many still do); did it matter whether or not this was the same as the northern Englishman's morte or the Scotsman's herling? Even the fish of North America suffered from the Old World's colloquial habits. British migrants to New England gave the name 'brook trout' to a fish that is biologically not a trout at all, but a char.

In the early 19th century everything changed. A surge of interest in natural history coincided with a new passion for travel. The up-bringing of the British gentleman had long required a Grand Tour of Europe; but during the Napoleonic Wars, a generation of gentlemen embarked on journeys around their own country. For angler-naturalists this meant a season

ABOVE
Lough Mask, in County Mayo, is one of Ireland's premier trout lakes.

RIGHT
A wild rainbow trout.

THE TROUT'S LIFE CYCLE

All trout are born in freshwater, usually in flowing river water or in a lake close to a feeder or outflow stream. Trout eggs cannot develop in sea-water and they require a good through-flow of oxygenated water if they are to develop. After a period of 30 or more days, depending on water temperature, the eggs hatch into alevins, embryonic fish that retain the remains of the yolk sac and continue to live deep in the gravel redd. Once the supply of yolk has been exhausted the alevin becomes a fry, and swims up through the gravel and starts to feed.

The tiny fry grows quickly and soon begins to attain the appearance of a trout, but with ovoid markings down its sides. These markings, known as parr-markings, give the name 'parr' to the young trout stage. The word parr derives from the Old English word for finger: such small trout are sometimes known as 'fingerlings' and the parr marks as 'fingermarks'. How long the trout remains as a parr depends to a large extent on the amount of food in the water: it may be anything from one year to four years. At this stage, sea-going varieties of trout assume silver coats and head downstream. They are then known as 'smolts'. Trout that spend their entire lives in freshwater assume adult coloration without going through the smolt stage.

Trout come into breeding condition at any age from three years upward and then embark on what, for the non-river varieties, can be the hazardous journey to the spawning grounds. Those that feed in shoals—the sea-going trout and many lake forms—make their runs up the river in loose shoals. In many cases, these trout either do not feed at all or else take in very little food while they are in the river. They must therefore survive the journey on the food reserves they have built up on their feeding grounds: reserves of oil and protein in their muscles. By contrast, river trout, which tend to be solitary feeders, remain solitary as they move to the spawning grounds. They make their way slowly, stopping at intervals to take up 'lies' in the river and feed.

The trout adopt their mates in the spawning areas, usually shallow water flowing over pea-sized gravel. With a sweep of the tail, the females cut channels known as redds in the gravel and deposit the eggs, which the male fertilizes with 'milt' before covering up the redd. Once spawning is completed the trout (now known as 'kelts') move quickly downstream, often in poor physical condition and considerably darker in colour. For sea trout, the journey may take several weeks and, though some kelts may take some food, mortality is high. Lake trout, too, may be severely weakened; but many varieties of river trout will resume feeding normally as soon as breeding is completed. They will even devour the eggs of other trout and salmon that have been washed from the redds.

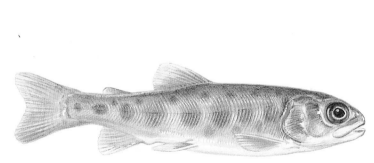

LEFT
A trout fry with its parr marks developing. Some weeks after the young trout fry finally exhausts the food supply of its own original egg yolk, it acquires a series of oval markings along the body. When these markings are fully developed then the fry will be a parr.

Field study/pencil and wash

RIGHT
At Poolewe, in northwest Scotland, freshwater flows into the sea. Thousands of trout smolts pass seawards through the loch in late spring.

RIGHT
A sea trout smolt. This specimen was taken from the headwaters of a river that cannot be reached by sea trout: its parents were river brown trout whose genes resulted in some of their progeny becoming sea trout.

Field study/pencil and wash

combing the wilder regions of the British Isles. In North America a parallel process was underway, as naturalists eagerly sought out the undocumented wildlife of the New World.

The angler-naturalists gradually unravelled the life history of the trout. They discovered that some trout migrate to sea, like the salmon, but return to their natal rivers to breed. They found that trout which spend their whole lives in rivers tend to be solitary, while lake trout often feed in shoals. And by dint of close and persistent observation of trout in their environment, they realised that all trout change considerably in size and coloration as they mature and reach breeding age. For the first time it was recognized that the distinctive features of young river trout (known as parr), sea trout before breeding (smolts) and adults returning to the sea from the spawning grounds (kelts) marked the stages in a single life cycle.

When these names were first applied, by the English and Scots in the 15th–17th centuries, it was believed that parr, smolt and kelt were separate varieties of fish. The Victorian naturalists demonstrated the error of this identification, and went on to make comparisons in meticulous detail of trout from different regions and waters. They found that the trout of certain lakes were markedly different in colour, anatomy and behaviour from the trout of all other lakes. They took detailed measurements of river trout, proving that some rivers produce larger trout than others. They demonstrated that where two or more forms of trout share the same waters, they still remain segregated in their feeding and spawning habits. And concluding that the term 'trout' embraced a huge range of fish, they adopted the Linnaean system of classification and gave each variety a scientific name.

The causes of variation within species were explained by Charles Darwin in his book *On the Origin of Species*, published in 1859. There Darwin argued that varieties within a species or closely related species have evolved from a common ancestor. Three contributory factors are essential to this process. First, the original ancestral stock must have had innate genetic variation. Second, the ancestral stock must have been split up into several discrete populations by geographical barriers. Third, each of these populations must have had different pressures put upon them by living in their isolated regions. So, with time, genetic differences have accumulated in each population: the result of 'natural selection' adapting each population to its geographical niche. The outcome of this process is that each population eventually becomes a separate variety or 'subspecies' of the parent species, or even accumulates sufficient genetic differences to merit being given full-species status.

Darwin's work provided the stimulus for other naturalists to travel all over the world on the quest for more evidence to support the evolutionary theory. Every species or group of similar species was carefully analysed; even the most minor and subtle features were seized on. These naturalists—referred to as 'splitters' by modern biologists because of their eagerness to split one species into many—found an excellent source of material in the world's wild trout.

Men like William Yarrell (author of *A History of British Fishes*, 1859), the Reverend W. Houghton (*British Freshwater Fishes*, 1879), and Dr. A. Günter, a scientist at the British Museum and author of an *Introduction to the Study of Fishes* (1880) produced a huge list of Old World trout species. In the United States and Canada the same work was carried out by David Starr Jordan (co-author with B. W. Evermann of *The Fishes of North and Middle America*, 1896–1898) and a series of

RIGHT
Yellowstone Lake, Wyoming, in the first frost of the fall. This lake has its own variety of cutthroat.

angler-naturalists including J. O. Snyder, who investigated the Pyramid Lake region of Nevada, and S. E. Meek, who explored the Olympic Mountains in Washington State.

The splitters gave names to literally scores of trout 'species'. In the British Isles there was the Loch Leven trout *Salmo levenensis*, the gillaroo *Salmo stomachicus*, the black-finned trout *Salmo nigripinnis*, the ferox trout *Salmo ferox*, the sea trout *Salmo fario* and so on. In Mexico, the United States and Canada the trout of almost every lake and river system were given their own special scientific names. Each variety was meticulously observed and described. Many were well known to anglers and, indeed, some still are. The Welsh still have their sewin and in Ireland keen anglers troll the deepest lakes for the ferox trout. In British Columbia fishermen seek the Kamloops trout; in Washington State, Lake Crescent is still visited by anglers hoping to catch bluebacks and speckled trout; the rainbow trout of Eagle Lake in California are still called Eagle Lake Trout.

But the species-splitters were so keen that they brought their enthusiasm into disrepute by naming some quite ridiculous 'varieties'. There was the hog-backed trout of Bagail Llyn, a lake on the slopes of the Welsh mountain Plinlimmon, which was said to have a humped back rather like a perch. Then there was the deformed trout or bulldog trout of Loch Dow, in Scotland: this had a shortened upper jaw and a protruding lower jaw. Most ludicrous of all was the croaking trout of the Carraclwddy Pools in Wales. 'A writer who visited the pools some years ago as an investigator avouches the croaking. "When first taken," he says, "and even when they have been in the basket for some time, they do decidedly utter a peculiar croak."' (H. C. Pennell, *Fishing: Salmon and Trout*, 1885).

The 'splitters' lost credibility in scientific circles and were replaced, early in the 20th century, by the 'clumpers': naturalists

THE LOCH LEVEN TROUT

Following the retreat of the ice sheets from northern Britain some 10,000 years ago, a massive block of ice was left stranded just north of the Firth of Forth in what is now southeast Scotland. As the climate slowly warmed, the ice melted, and its water cut a river into the Forth at Largo Bay. The lake that now fills the depression made by this gigantic block of ice has become the most famous trout water in the world: Loch Leven.

Since the middle of the 19th century, the Loch Leven strain of brown trout has been transported to many regions that were formerly far beyond the range of any trout species: Argentina, the Indian subcontinent, the Falkland Islands, Australia and New Zealand. In North America it now lives alongside the native rainbow and cutthroat trout. And in fisheries throughout Europe, trout farmers take pride in the knowledge that their brown trout originate from the Loch Leven strain.

Presumably Loch Leven was colonised soon after the ice melted, by trout from the sea running through the Forth and the River Leven. Over thousands of years the trout population became specially adapted to life in the loch. They acquired a coloration that presumably camouflages them from predators better than any other. They became adapted to feeding on the invertebrates with which the loch abounds, especially crustaceans such as the freshwater shrimp and planktonic *Daphnia*, which are rich in carotenoids and produce the appetising redness of the trout flesh.

A freshly-caught Loch Leven trout can quite easily be distinguished from trout caught elsewhere. Early scientists considered it a separate species. Before Dr Günter and the Reverend Houghton referred to the Loch Leven trout as *Salmo levenensis*, a Dr Parnell named it *Salmo caecifer* because of the large number of 'caecae' or appendices that it had in its gut system.

However, when stocks of Loch Leven trout are taken and introduced into other waters they lose some of the characteristics that they have in their natal loch. They interbreed freely with any other brown trout in the water, and very quickly become almost indistinguishable from the trout native in the lake or river. Even in fish farms where the strain is kept isolated from others, some of the Loch Leven characteristics can soon be lost; especially the colour. So to see a Loch Leven trout at its best there is no choice: you have to go to Loch Leven.

The quantities of trout caught on rod and line, all on fly, from Loch Leven are quite immense for the size of the water. Less than 20,000 in the season is a bad season, 30,000 a reasonable one, 40,000 a very good season. In 1929 it is recorded that 53,605 trout were taken at an average of 15 trout per acre. Considering that the average weight is close to the pound mark, it is clear that the loch is a very productive fishery.

The loch does not, however, produce big trout in quantity and anything over the 5 lbs mark must be considered exceptional. As recently as 1980 one of 6 lbs 3 oz was taken by W. Hatten on a McLeod's Olive Fly; and in 1983, Eugene Grube had one of 5 lbs 12 oz. But pride of place must go to Colonel Scott's fish of 9 lbs 13 oz, caught on 8 September 1911: to this day it still resides in a glass case in the Fishery Centre at Kinross Pier.

In former centuries, Loch Leven was about four miles long and three miles wide. But in December 1830 a

LOCH LEVEN BROWN TROUT
Salmo trutta trutta

drainage scheme was completed that dropped the water level of the loch by up to nine feet and reduced its area by almost a quarter. The scheme also involved cutting a new channel for the outflowing River Leven and creating sluices to control the flow of water from the loch.

The appearance of the loch before the drainage can be gauged by the visitor at the old churchyard of Kinross. Originally the water lapped at the foot of the churchyard wall. On Castle Island, when Mary, Queen of Scots, was imprisoned there in the 1560s, the loch reached the battlements. Today the loch reveals seven islands, but prior to the drainage there were but four: St Serf's, Castle, the Reed Bower and Roy's Folly. Most of the loch is now very shallow, with the exceptions of two 60-foot holes to the east of Scart Island and around the western and southern sides of St Serf's. Before 1830 the large area known as "The Shallows" was more than twice its present depth.

This massive alteration has had major effects on the fish populations of Loch Leven. Salmon, and possibly sea trout, ran the old River Leven: they are gone. So too is the char which, presumably, could not tolerate the shallower water. The pike is also extinct here, but not because of the drainage: it was exterminated to protect the trout stocks (in 1903 14,000 pike were removed by netting).

ABOVE
Loch Leven and Castle Island, seen from the old churchyard at Kinross.

RIGHT
An angler's map shows the banks and depths of Loch Leven. The straight, dotted lines mark two favourite drifts for fishermen: due south from the Old Manse to 'the Elbow', a stretch of water by Scart Island; and southeast from the Elbow towards St Serfs, the biggest island in the lake.

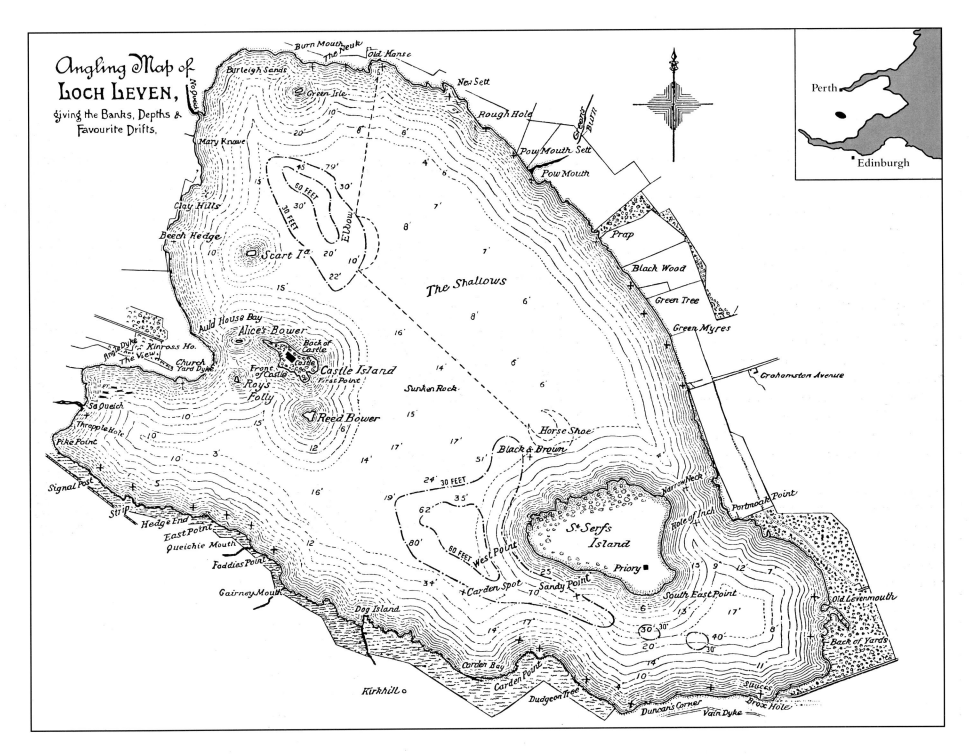

Angling Map of
LOCH LEVEN,
giving the Banks, Depths &
Favourite Drifts,

Perth

Edinburgh

Burn Mouth
The Neuk
Old Manse
Burleigh Sands
Green Isle
New Sett
Rough Hole
Green Burn
Pow Mouth Sett
Pow Mouth
No Queich
Mary Knowe
45   79'
60 FEET   30'
30 FEET   30'
Clay Hills   Elbow
Beech Hedge   20'
10'   22'
Scart Iª
15'
Prap
Black Wood
Green Tree
Green Myres
The Shallows
Auld House Bay
Alice's Bower
Angle Dyke   Back of Castle
Kinross Ho.
The View   Castle
Church   Front   Castle Island
Yard Dyke   of Castle   First Point
Sunken Rock
Ray's Folly
Sd Queich   Reed Bower   Horse Shoe
Thropple Hole   Black & Brown
Pike Point   Narrow Neck
Portmoak Point
Signal Post   30 FEET   St Serfs
Strip   62   35'   Island   Hole of Inch
Hedge End   80'   60 FEET   West Point
East Point   Priory
Queichie Mouth   Carden Spot   Sandy Point   South East Point
Faddies Point   Old Levenmouth
Gairney Mouth   Back of Yards
Dog Island   Sluices
Carden Bay   Brox Hole
Kirkhill   Carden Point
Dudgeon Tree   Duncan's Corner
Vain Dyke

Grahamston Avenue

who insist that the different forms are merely variations within a species and do not warrant special names. For instance, in 1911 C. Tate Regan (in *The Freshwater Fishes of the British Isles*) commented of the supposed trout species of Britain that, 'All these are here regarded as pertaining to one variable species'; biologically, no real difference could be detected.

The orthodox view is still that of the 'clumpers'. In 1967 W. E. Frost and M. E. Brown, in *The Trout*, concluded that the trout of northern Europe is a 'single polytypic species': meaning a single species exhibiting many forms. This was reiterated by A. Wheeler of the British Museum (Natural History) in his book *The Fishes of the British Isles and North-west Europe* (1969). In North America a recent review by R. J. Behnke *Monograph of the Native Trouts of the Genus Salmo of Western North America* (1979) similarly rationalised the situation in the New World trout.

Today, wild trout throughout the world are divided into just three species: *Salmo trutta*, *Salmo gairdneri* and *Salmo clarki*. *Salmo* indicates the genus or group to which all the trout belong: the same group as the Atlantic salmon (*Salmo salar*). Within that genus, *Salmo trutta* comprises all the brown trout of Europe and Western Asia, while the wild trout of North America are divided into the rainbow trout *Salmo gairdneri* and the cutthroat trout *Salmo clarki*. Some other fish are also called 'trout', notably the brook trout of North America. However, biologically speaking the brook trout is a char and belongs to the genus *Salvelinus*, and not *Salmo*. It is therefore better given its alternative English name, the speckled char.

The arguments about which local populations can be called subspecies and which are mere varieties rage on, but there is broad acceptance of the main divisions within the three species of trout. Most naturalists accept the classification proposed by the Russian scientist L. S. Berg for the Old World trout of Europe and Asia:

Salmo trutta trutta the trout of North and West Europe
Salmo trutta aralensis the trout of the Aral Sea and River Oxus
Salmo trutta carpione the trout of Lake Garda, Italy
Salmo trutta caspius the trout of the Caspian Sea basin
Salmo trutta labrax the trout of the Black Sea basin
Salmo trutta macrostigma the trout of the Mediterranean basin

Each of the subspecies *trutta aralensis*, *caspius* and *labrax* includes river, lake and migratory (sea-going) forms. *Salmo carpione* is thought to have evolved from the Mediterranean subspecies *macrostigma*, which occurs in lakes and rivers but lacks a sea-going population.

New World trout remain the subject of intense debate, but the following is probably the best accepted classification of the cutthroat trout:

Salmo clarki clarki the cutthroat of the Pacific coast
Salmo clarki lewisi the West-slope cutthroat or Montana black spot
Salmo clarki bouvieri the Yellowstone cutthroat
Salmo clarki henshawi the trout of the Lahontan basin
Salmo clarki seleniris the Paiute trout
Salmo clarki utah the trout of the Bonneville region
Salmo clarki pleuriticus the Colorado cutthroat
Salmo clarki virginalis the Rio Grande cutthroat
Salmo clarki stomias the greenback cutthroat
Salmo clarki macdonaldi the yellow-finned cutthroat

Of these subspecies of cutthroat trout all have lake and river populations, but only one, *Salmo clarki clarki*, the cutthroat of

RIGHT
The trout ancestor, Eosalmo driftwoodensis: *a reconstruction from a fossil found at Driftwood Creek in British Columbia. Over the last forty million years our present forms of trout and salmon have evolved from a fish like this. Compared with modern trout,* Eosalmo *was a short, deep-bodied fish, with a huge dorsal fin and a primitive skull structure.*

Reconstruction/pencil

the Pacific coast, also has a population that migrates to sea.

Some authors have suggested two other subspecies of cutthroat trout. *Salmo clarki carmichaeli* is the name given to the cutthroat of Jackson Hole and part of the Snake River system. However, its range in western Wyoming is completely surrounded by that of the Yellowstone cutthroat, from which this population has few clear-cut differences. *Salmo clarki humboldtensis* has been suggested for the cutthroats of central and northern Nevada. Since they differ only slightly from their near neighbours, the Lahontan trout, many biologists consider them a variety of the subspecies *henshawi*.

Patrick C. Trotter, in his book *Cutthroat* (1987) suggested that the scarce tiny cutthroat trout of Whitehorse and Willow creeks, in the desert region of southeastern Oregon might also be worthy of subspecific status; likewise the extinct or near-extinct cutthroat of the desert country of the Alvord Basin. Others consider them varieties which have become adapted to the harsh conditions of their home range over the past few thousand years. The question that needs to be answered is: if a pair of tiny trout was taken from Willow or Whitehorse creek, or from the Alvord Basin (if one could be found), would their progeny—raised in captivity—retain all the characters that make the wild fish so distinct?

The classification of the varieties of rainbow trout is currently subject to much investigation, argument and review. A compromise might reasonably be:

Salmo gairdneri gairdneri the river rainbow trout
Salmo gairdneri irideus the coastal rainbow trout
Salmo gairdneri gilberti
Salmo gairdneri whitei] forms of the golden trout
Salmo gairdneri aguabonita] of California

Salmo gairdneri newberryi the Klamath River trout
Salmo gairdneri apache the Apache trout of Arizona
Salmo gairdneri gilae the rare Gila trout of the desert regions of southwest USA
Salmo gairdneri chryogaster the Mexican golden trout

Most of these forms of the rainbow trout have both lake and river varieties. Only the coastal rainbow trout has a variety that migrates seawards, the Pacific steelhead trout.

Some scientists consider the Mexican golden trout to be a species in its own right, a status that was afforded until quite recently also to the Californian golden trout, and to the Gila and Apache trouts.

The origins of all these numerous forms of wild trout can be traced back some 70 million years, to when the whitefish and the line that would eventually lead to the trout split off from a common ancestor. The earliest known fossil member of this line, known as *Protothymallus*, was found in Miocene deposits in Germany. During the next 30 million years the grayling separated from the line, and we find the emergence of the forerunner of the genus *Salmo* in the form of an Eocene fossil *Eosalmo*. Sometime in the next 30 million years two side branches split from the trout-salmon line: one of these was the branch that gave rise to the chars *Salvelinus*, a group that is widespread throughout the arctic and northern temperate parts of the world; the other led to the huchen *Hucho* which exists now only in Europe.

About 10 million years ago, a vast geological movement in the Earth's crust led to the formation of the Pacific basin, and

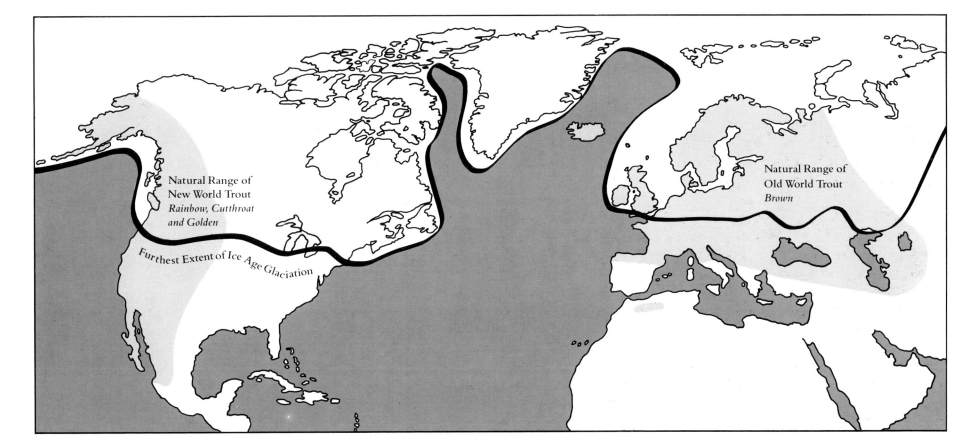

Natural Range of
New World Trout
*Rainbow, Cutthroat
and Golden*

Furthest Extent of Ice Age Glaciation

Natural Range of
Old World Trout
Brown

ABOVE

A map showing the furthest extent of the ice sheets during the Pleistocene era, and the current range of wild trout. During maximum glaciation 15,000 years ago trout were excluded from much of their present range in Canada and northwest USA, Iceland, the British Isles and northern mainland Eurasia. When the ice retreated, sea-going trout recolonised freshwater lakes and rivers.

separated the New World from the Old World trout and salmon. The genus *Salmo* has been split into two 'subgenera' to indicate this division. The Old World, or Atlantic, trout and salmon are members of the subgenus *Salmo*, and the New World, or Pacific, salmon and trout belong to the subgenus *Parasalmo*. In evolutionary terms, the brown trout is more closely related to the Atlantic salmon than to the cutthroat or rainbow trouts, and the cutthroat and rainbow trouts are closer to the Pacific salmon than to the brown trout.

The Ice Ages, which began about $2\frac{1}{2}$–3 million years ago, had a powerful impact on both New and Old World trout. Much of the northern hemisphere was subjected to a series of alternating cold and warm periods. During the cold periods the arctic ice cap advanced far to the south, blanketing trout homelands in North America, Asia and Europe. During the warm phases the ice withdrew. The last ice advance reached its southernmost extent about 15,000 years ago and then, about 10,000 years ago, retreated rapidly. During this era of successive ice advances and retreats, known as the Pleistocene period, the forms of trout we see today evolved. As the ice advanced it forced the existing trout stocks to retreat from much of their range, and split up the surviving stocks into a number of ice-free areas or refuges. Now conditions were ripe for change: a genetically variable trout stock was split up into a number of isolated units, and left for several thousands of years.

It was probably in the earliest part of the Pleistocene that the Atlantic salmon split from the brown trout line, and the cutthroat trout separated from the rainbow. It may have been early in the Pleistocene that the Mexican golden trout and rare Gila and Apache trouts emerged, for some authorities consider that they have evolved sufficient differences from the rainbow trout group to be considered worthy of full species status.

However, varieties such as the Kamloops trout of British Columbia, the cutthroat of Yellowstone, and the trout of Loch Leven probably emerged towards the end of the Ice Ages.

In the past 10,000 years, since the last retreat of the arctic ice cap, the trout has continued to evolve. Wherever trout are isolated from other populations—whether in a lake or river system—they have adapted to that particular waterway. Some populations have acquired unique characteristics, making them easily identifiable. In such cases biologists have had to decide whether to classify the population as a subspecies, or merely as a 'variety'.

The main problem scientists face in identifying and classifying trout, is that the features that are compared are often quite trivial and highly variable. And the difficulty is exacerbated by a simple biological rule: the appearance and structure of each fish is the result of the interaction of genetics and the environment. Thus the scientist has to judge, from evidence which is very hard to assess, which features are genetically produced, and therefore warrant formal classification, and which are the product of the trout's environment. Size is a classic example. An individual trout may have genes that will promote rapid growth; but if the waters the fish inhabits do not provide enough food, it will not reach its full potential, and the nature of these genes will be hidden. Likewise colour: although the trout's genes will to some extent determine its coloration, the background colours and degree of spotting of trout can vary considerably according to the water they live in and the food they eat.

In an attempt to remove these environmental influences, many scientists based their analysis on certain quite precise anatomical features such as the number and arrangement of the trout's scales. Such features, which are termed 'meristic', were

RIGHT
Loch Maree, in northwest
Scotland, one of the finest
Atlantic sea trout lakes,
fills the floor of a valley
gouged out by glacial action
more than 10,000 years ago.

believed to remain quite fixed no matter how the environment varied. Yet experiments have proved that even these structural features can be the result of environmental influences. The North American Kamloops trout was initially classified as a subspecies on the meristic feature of scale counts, but later experimentation showed that this number varied according to the water temperature when the scales were being formed. Similarly, the trout of Loch Leven in Scotland is considered a distinct form of trout that can be identified by its colour and meristic features. Yet when the Loch Leven trout has been introduced elsewhere in the world, its colour and its meristic measurements have become altered by the new environment.

Moreover, because of the genetic similarities within a species, there is often a great overlap in meristic measurements between the subspecies and varieties. Thus the identification of trout by meristic features must be largely a statistical assessment: one population can be said to differ significantly, as far as these features are concerned, from other populations. It is often impossible to say that an individual is definitely of that population unless its origin is known.

The 'clumpers' argument, that the apparently different varieties of trout were merely the result of environmental factors, seemed until recently to be conclusive. But the latest biochemical research suggests that in many cases the trout from one water are indeed genetically different (possibly quite subtly different) from the same species of trout in another water.

In North America Robert Behnke of the Colorado State University and C. L. Hubbs and L. C. Hubbs, amongst others, have used chromosomal analysis as well as computer analysis of meristic features to illustrate the genetically discrete nature of many New World trout varieties. And in a paper published in 1981 in the *Journal of Fish Biology*, A. Ferguson and F. M. Mason of The Queen's University of Belfast described how they had used the most modern method of gel electrophoresis (genetic finger-printing) to show that the ferox, gillaroo and sonaghen trout of Ireland's Lough Melvin 'represent genetically distinct and reproductively isolated populations'. This was an exciting development because it lent modern scientific credence to at least some of the 'splitters' species that had been dismissed as trivial varieties by the 'clumpers'. Since many of these wild trout populations face the threat of extinction by water pollution and other man-made hazards, re-classification could be crucial to their survival.

For the angler and the conservationist, scientific status is not the real issue. No matter what classification a population of trout is given, it remains a wild population that has become adapted to its own environment over several thousand years, and is worthy of protection. But as the pressures on the environment become more and more threatening, science and conservation have become intertwined. We hope that the latest studies will start a new appraisal of trout varieties, and provoke greater public awareness of their qualities.

THE LOUGH MELVIN TROUT

Though not the most famous of the Irish loughs, Lough Melvin is certainly the most special so far as wild trout are concerned, for the waters are inhabited by five different varieties: the brown trout, sea trout, gillaroo, ferox and one form unique to this lake: the sonaghen. These varieties share the lough with other native fish including the Atlantic salmon, char and eel, as well as the perch and rudd, which were introduced by man.

Lying on the border of the Republic of Ireland and the United Kingdom province of Northern Ireland, the lough is about 7½ miles long and up to 2 miles wide with its long axis lying east-west. Water leaves the western end of the lake to flow down to the Atlantic through the Drowes River and is replaced by the inflowing rivers—the Tullymore, Roogagh, County, Ballagh and Glenaniff—that drain the surrounding countryside and enter the lough on the eastern shores.

Over much of the western half and around the skerries and islands of the northeast, the lake is quite shallow at up to about 33 feet deep. By contrast, in the wide open basin of the southeast, between Ross Point and Breffni Pier, and extending as a trench northwestwards between the islands of Inisheher and Inishmean and the northern shore the water is much deeper, reaching a maximum depth of 150 feet.

To the south of Lough Melvin the land rises rapidly through woodland and rough pasture to hills reaching over 1300 feet, while on the east and northern sides the catchment consists mostly of lower-lying pasture and woodland. The water that drains this area and enters the rivers and thence the lough has very little added in the way

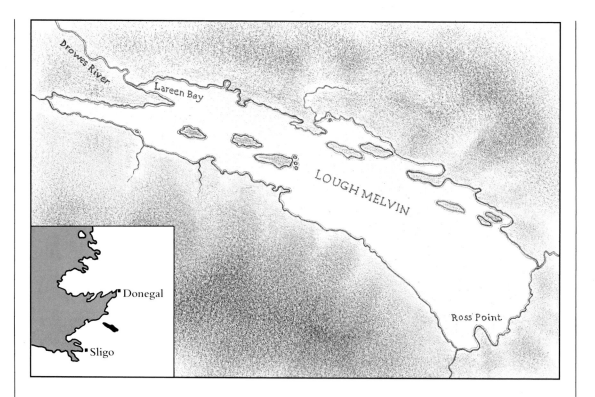

of artificial fertilizers: most of the mineral salts in the lake are acquired naturally from the soil.

Like the other Irish loughs, Melvin was formed during or after the last Ice Age, so the wild trout must have colonized its waters via the sea and the Drowes River. Today, sea trout are quite scarce in Lough Melvin compared with the four lake varieties; in some Irish loughs such as Corrib and the Scottish lochs they are abundant.

The four forms of lake trout in Lough Melvin have been the subject of a recent (1977–1984) study by Andrew Ferguson and his co-workers in the Department of Zoology

ABOVE

Lough Melvin, on the border between Northern Ireland and the Republic.

RIGHT

Lough Melvin's three wild trout varieties show considerable differences in size, shape and colour.

Comparative study/watercolour

Ferox Trout *Salmo trutta trutta*

Gillaroo Trout *Salmo trutta trutta*

Sonaghen Trout *Salmo trutta trutta*

at The Queen's University of Belfast. After examining hundreds of specimens, and applying the technique of gel electrophoresis ('genetic finger-printing') they concluded that the gillaroo, sonaghen and ferox constitute three genetically distinct varieties of trout; while the form that has for years been referred to as 'brown trout' appears genetically to be either gillaroo or sonaghen that has not, for some reason, attained its full characteristics.

So different genetically are these three varieties that Ferguson and his colleagues suggested that they could be considered full trout species.

The genetic differences between the three varieties are reinforced by ecological separation: the gillaroo, sonaghen and ferox occur in different parts of the lough and feed on different sorts of prey; and they also spawn in different areas so that there is no interbreeding between the three forms. All the gillaroos spawn in the River Drowes or Loreen Bay. All the sonaghens breed separately in the small feeder streams of the lough, especially the Ballagh, County and Tullymore rivers. And the ferox trout move from the lough into the River Glenaniff where most of the Melvin Atlantic salmon also spawn.

The other large loughs of Ireland have subtle, but important differences from Melvin: their fish stocks have been more tampered with by man. In some cases this has been quite inadvertent: more intense agriculture in the catchment area, notably the addition of large and regular doses of artificial fertilizers which are readily leached into the lake, has enriched the water, increasing the production of plant and animal life, and affecting the trout population.

In other cases the interference has been conscious. In some loughs over-fishing (especially with nets) with or

without artificial stocking has certainly spoilt the genetic structure of the trout populations. The effect has been exacerbated by adding a wider range of introduced fish species to most loughs: especially the pike. This fish-eating predator, which is very fond of salmonids, is likely to have affected the structure of the trout populations in many lakes.

Gillaroos (or, at least, trout resembling gillaroos) still occur in some other lakes, such as Lough Conn in County Mayo. So do ferox-type trout. Sea trout, together with salmon, still run from the Atlantic into many loughs. But if

sonaghens ever existed in the other big Irish loughs, they certainly do not today. These other big loughs contain large numbers of brown trout, and the productivity of the water results in a rapid growth rate; so the angling is quite spectacular, attracting visitors from around the world.

CHAPTER TWO

WILD TROUT IN RIVERS

Almost all trout spend part of their lives in rivers and streams. Even trout that migrate to sea—the steelhead and sea-run cutthroat of North America and the Atlantic sea trout of Europe—are born in rivers, where they may spend a year or more as parr before making their journey downriver to salt water; when fully grown, the urge to reproduce drives them back to their natal rivers. Similarly, lake trout may spend the bulk of their lives in still water but most are born and return to breed in the lake's feeder and outflow streams.

The true river trout, however, never leaves its native river system, and may indeed spend much of its life in precise locations or 'lies' in the river. These lies are chosen by the trout because they provide some shelter: possibly a swathe of river weed, or a deep hole under a high bank, or by a large boulder, or the fast streamy neck of a river pool, or beneath overhanging tree branches. Lies are also chosen by the river trout because they provide the fish with a steady supply of insect food that is being carried down the river.

This is one major difference in behaviour between river trout and trout that feed in lakes, estuaries or at sea. The latter must often swim some distance during the course of a day in their search for food, and because many pairs of eyes are better than one, most lake, estuary and sea trout feed in shoals. Not the river trout; the stream brings the food to the trout. But because of the irregularity of the flow down a stream, due to the flow being broken by large boulders, weirs, the meandering of the river banks and so on, some parts of the stream will carry more food than others. The trout compete for the best positions: the more food and the better the cover provided by a lie, then usually the bigger the trout in that lie. An older, larger trout will vigorously defend its lie against a lesser trout.

All river trout anglers can cite examples of such lies from their own rivers. Lies where there will be a good trout. Lies that often give the trout the sort of cover that makes catching them difficult. Lies that, once a big trout is removed, are never left vacant for long: another trout, perhaps not quite as large as the earlier occupant, will soon move in having abandoned its previous, lesser lie. It is as though there is a peck order based on the trout lies on each stretch of river. When the trout at the top of the peck order disappears (by dying, or being caught by man or another predator) all the other trout move up one place.

In *Minor Tactics of the Chalk Stream* (1910), the famous angler-naturalist G. E. M. Skues wrote of one trout which seemed never to leave its lie.

> 'She was called Aunt Sally because everyone felt bound to have a shy at her. Her coign of vantage was near the bottom of the water, where the fishery begins, and her irritating "pip, pip," as she took fly after fly in the culvert that was her home was too much for the nerves of nine anglers out of ten. This was the fastness in which Aunt Sally had taken up her abode, and throughout the spring and summer had defied all efforts to dislodge her.'

There are many similar tales of river trout, often known personally by name, that inhibit quite distinct lies: hatch pools, beneath bridges, below overhanging branches, above and below weirs, and so on. Every time the angler passes he raises his hat, wishes the trout 'Good Morning!', makes a token cast at his old friend, and then moves on upstream. So it goes for the whole season from April to September when he waves cheerio to the river and wishes his finny friend farewell. And often, on the first day of the next season, our angler returns to the river. There, in the same place, is the trout. 'A Happy New Year' he shouts as he raises his hat and prepares for the token cast!

Contrary to angling myth, however, no river trout remain permanently in one lie, year after year; in certain water conditions and on some rivers even a well-established trout may have two lies: a feeding lie and a resting lie. During high summer, when the river is very low and the light bright through the day, the shallow flow which produces a potentially good food supply may be dangerous during the daytime. In the glare of the bright sunlight streaming through the shallow clear water the trout may be easily seen, yet unable to see potential predators approaching. Unlike humans, trout cannot contract the pupil of the eye to reduce the glare of bright light. In such conditions the trout may therefore seek cover in the shade of riverside vegetation.

Come evening, as the light fails, the trout will leave the cool dark daytime lie and swim into the shallow streamy water to feed, under cover of darkness, on the evening hatches of mayflies and the night hatches of sedges. During drought conditions on Scotland's River Nith, one large brown trout (that could be identified by a very pale pectoral fin) was followed on seven consecutive evenings for nearly 200 yards, as it swam from its daytime lie amongst the roots of a riverside alder to its evening lie beside a boulder in four inches of open water. In July 1975 a tributary of the Madison River in Wyoming seemed fishless until dusk, when the cutthroat trout moved from their daytime lies in the deeper pools to feeding lies in the shallow, faster water.

Through the year many river trout move even further afield. The upper reaches of spate streams often seem devoid of trout through the spring, when the fish are feeding lower down the river. A visit to the river may be marked by the year's first large hatches of flies, but not one fish breaks the surface; in June or July the same length of stream is alive with trout. However, the major movement of river trout tends to occur in winter, between October and April, when the trout move on to the redds to spawn. For some trout, this means a short trip to the nearest patch of fine gravel. For many it may be an upstream journey of several miles, from the deep silty pools of the lower reaches to the fast gravel-strewn runs of the headwater streams. Even trout that remain faithful to one particular lie for most of the year, will leave that lie to spawn.

The notion that trout commonly remain faithful to a particular lie is therefore quite unfounded. The vast majority of river trout move from lie to lie as they ascend the peck order, sometimes passing from one length of river to another, even swimming the whole length of the river system during the course of a year. Equally mythical is the much vaunted intelligence of wild trout in rivers. When anglers refer to trout as being educated or wily they flatter fish whose intellect is similar to that of a farmyard chicken; possibly even less.

Nevertheless, to survive by eating and avoid being eaten trout have evolved a highly acute set of sensory organs. They have a system of nerve endings in the lateral line that can detect the approach of danger through vibrations in the water. Watch a trout in the river while you stamp on the bank: though it may not see you, its lateral line will warn the trout that you are there. Its fins may quiver; it may sidle under a patch of weed; it may even flee.

Trout also have remarkably keen eyesight which enables them to scrutinise potential food items and to see predators approach. Many anglers, thwarted despite carefully selecting a trout's favourite fly and casting with consummate skill, have credited the fish with intelligence. But it is more likely that the trout has actually seen the bend, point and eye of the hook, and

RIGHT
River trout 'on-the-fin'. The largest fish holds the best lie: a pool sheltered by overhanging branches, where the current carries most food.

Pastel and wash

THE RIVER BROWN TROUT

Although scientists recognise no genetic distinction between the brown trout, or 'brownie', and most other varieties of *Salmo trutta*, the Old World trout, many anglers and naturalists prefer to call it *Salmo trutta fario*, and distinguish not only between lake and river varieties, but between the trout of the lowland chalkstreams and the smaller fish of spate rivers. Although their lifestyle and behaviour are similar throughout most of their range, brown trout can vary considerably in size and coloration according to the waters they inhabit and the available food.

Most river brown trout spawn during early winter (November and December), migrating upstream to the shallow gravel runs of the main river or the tiny feeder streams. They then drop back downstream. Through the spring, summer and early autumn river brown trout remain very solitary fish, with each individual keeping to its lie and chasing off any lesser trout and parr that might intrude. From quite a small area, possibly only three yards long and one yard wide, they obtain all the food they require.

Much of their food is carried to them by the current: nymphs and larvae of aquatic insects that have been washed from the river bed, mature nymphs and pupae that rise from the riverbed to hatch at the water surface, and flies that have just hatched or been blown from the surrounding countryside on to the water surface. When the flow carries little potential food, river brown trout will grub around in the weed and gravel of their lies for freshwater shrimps, water hog-lice and immature nymphs and larvae.

The chalkstreams of England and northern Europe are far more productive than the spate rivers, and are considered by many to be the greatest of all trout rivers for the quality of their water. They are fed from massive underground reservoirs in the chalk downlands, so the flow is constant, save in the driest of summers; and except after the most torrential downpours the rivers rarely rise more than a few inches above their usual height. The riverbeds are very stable and support prolific growths of water weed, which in turn support a huge population of invertebrates on which the trout can feed.

In such waters the trout grow quickly, and in the past, could attain great size. In 1832, Stephen Oliver recorded a brownie from Yorkshire's Driffield Beck that was 31 inches in length and weighed 17 lbs (*Scenes and Recollections of Fly-Fishing*). The Linnaean Society of London reported a brown trout caught from the Wiltshire Avon at Salisbury in 1822 that scaled 25 lbs. The latter was kept alive: 'Mrs Powell, at the bottom of whose garden the fish was discovered, placed it in a pond, where it was fed and lived for four months.' Today the combined effects of heavy fishing pressure and artificial stocking make it highly unlikely that fish of these sizes will ever be caught again in chalkstreams. Today a 4 lb trout is considered a large fish.

RIGHT
A chalkstream brown trout. The heavy build, red spotting and red margin on the adipose fin are sure signs of good feeding in the most productive of trout streams.

Specimen study/watercolour

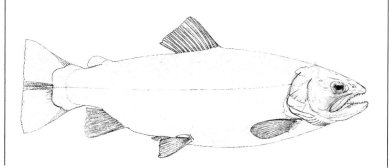

Working drawing/pencil

44

CHALKSTREAM BROWN TROUT
Salmo trutta trutta

Most of the other rivers and streams inhabited by the wild brown trout are rough, boulder-strewn torrents that drain regions dominated by high moor and mountain. After heavy rain, the huge volume of water draining through the steep slopes of the uplands will cause the river to rise rapidly. During periods of drought, these rivers shrink to mere trickles, exposing large banks of bare gravel. In the heat of the summer sun, or in winter weather, these banks may almost be sterilized of animal life.

During a powerful spate large numbers of the river invertebrates will be crushed by boulders rolling down the bed of the river; in winter spates a high proportion of trout redds will be smothered by shifting sand and gravel. Adult trout are not immune in severe spates: following one terrific flood more than a sackful of dead wild trout were collected from a short length of the tiny West Allen Burn in Northumberland.

Brown trout can often cope with such extremes of water flow. In droughts, when the river is low, they may become nocturnal in habit. They will seek the cool still pools beneath the shade of overhanging trees, or the aerated pools beneath waterfalls. Then, come sunset, they will move into the shallows to feed. When the river is in spate the trout will seek the quieter corners, often amongst flooded bankside vegetation, where the flow is less.

Spate streams produce relatively little food, so the trout grow slowly. In some of the moorland streams of northern England and Scotland, mature four-year-old trout may scale as little as $\frac{1}{4}$ lb, less than a fifth of their chalkstream relatives.

Spate river brown trout can vary considerably in appearance, and experienced naturalists and anglers have long distinguished between the wild trout of particular

ABOVE
Northumberland's West Allen River is a typical upland spate stream. In prolonged droughts it shrinks to a mere trickle; following heavy rain it is a raging torrent.

A rough-water brown trout. The heavily spotted coloration camouflages the fish when the stream is thin and clear, in high summer; the streamlined body and large tail fin help it cope with the swiftest spate.

Measured drawing/pencil and wash

rivers. In the third edition of his *A History of British Fishes* (1859) William Yarrell quotes the great Victorian angler Lord Home: 'There are two considerable streams in this country which take their rise at no great distance from each other, the Whitadder and the Blackadder, the latter tributary to the former. The Trout of Whitadder (White water) are a beautiful silvery fish, but good for nothing; those of the other dark, almost black, with bright orange fins, and their flesh excellent.'

LEFT
A fly floating downstream on the river surface vanishes in a swirl as a trout rises to intercept it.

the monofilament leader extending from the hook: features the natural fly does not have. It may be that trout which have been caught and released can grow wary of what they will and will not take from the water surface. They examine their food more carefully and are more likely to spot the deception in the angler's fly than fish that have never been caught before. But that reaction does not demonstrate intelligence. Exactly the same survival trait is exhibited by birds feeding on a bird table in a garden frequented by cats, or rabbits in a warren when a fox trots past.

Lake trout rarely enjoy the same reputation for intelligence as river trout. Yet this is almost certainly attributable to differences in the environment rather than the fish themselves. In a river the water flow acts as a conveyor belt carrying food to the trout in its lie; the trout selects what it wants from the stream. When the water is clear and carries plenty of food, the trout can afford to be choosy; angling is then at its most difficult. By contrast, lake trout cannot lie in one spot and wait for the food to arrive; they must actively seek food by hunting for it and possibly covering large distances in the process. Sometimes there may be a fall or hatch of flies at the lake surface that the trout will select. But large supplies of natural insects are much rarer on most trout lakes than on rivers. So, as it moves through the water, the lake trout will more often be prepared to take anything that might be edible.

The population density and the growth rate of wild trout in rivers depends largely on the availability of food and this in turn is directly related to the flow of water and the quantity of mineral salts (notably calcium carbonate) it contains. In chalkstreams, where a regular supply of water flows into the river from natural reservoirs in the surrounding chalk downs, and in lake-fed streams where the river level is kept fairly constant by the lake outflow, trout usually grow very quickly. By contrast, growth is usually much slower in upland spate streams, where the flow varies tremendously depending on the amount of rainfall.

This is clearly illustrated by the following data for wild brown trout, collected from rivers in the British Isles:

AVERAGE LENGTH OF RIVER BROWN TROUT AT AGE THREE YEARS

River	Ins	Cms
Test (Hampshire)	13.6	34
Kennet (Berkshire)	13.3	33
Avon (Wiltshire)	12.7	32
Black (Co. Galway)	12.1	31
Galway (Co. Galway)	11.8	30
Shannon (Co. Tipperary)	10.4	26
Aire (Yorkshire)	10.0	25
Eden (Cumbria)	8.0	20
Lune (Cumbria)	7.6	19
South Tyne (Northumberland)	6.2	16
Pennine Beck (Lancashire)	4.5	11

(Data from W. E. Frost & M. E. Brown, *The Trout*, 1967 and personal study)

The Test, Kennet and Avon are typical chalkstreams; the Irish Black, Galway and Shannon and the Yorkshire Aire are largely lake-fed. In these the combination of good flow rates and high productivity of trout foods results in rapid trout growth. The other four streams are rain-fed spate streams where the flow fluctuates widely from a spate-flood following a period of heavy rain to a mere trickle during a prolonged drought in summer.

Chalk rivers and lake-fed streams in limestone countryside almost invariably produce richer food stocks for the trout than spate streams or rivers draining acid moorlands. This is partly because the high concentration of mineral salts in chalk and limestone streams allows plants to flourish, and thus provides an abundance of food and cover for the invertebrates on which the trout feed. By contrast spate and acid streams tend to have less plant life and a smaller population of invertebrates. Fluctuations in water flow in spate rivers have damaging effects on the plant life. During prolonged droughts, large areas of river bed may dry out; heavy rainfall can produce torrents that pound the river bed by moving boulders and shingle. Few plants can survive such treatment, which ultimately means less food for the trout of spate rivers.

Rivers must be clean and cool if they are to support a good head of wild trout. This is often taken to mean that the oxygen level must be adequate; but the water must also be free from poisonous metal salts. In many regions of the world, mining spoil or industrial processes have released lead, mercury, cadmium and other heavy metal salts into well-oxygenated streams. Entire populations of freshwater plants and animals, including the wild trout, have been killed. Organic materials can be equally damaging. Where sewage effluent from outfalls, or faeces from wading cattle, or finely divided trash from lumber operations, or washings from paper mills enter the water, the oxygen level will fall because bacteria feed on this organic material and use up oxygen as they do so. The more of these organic pollutants, the more bacterial action and the lower

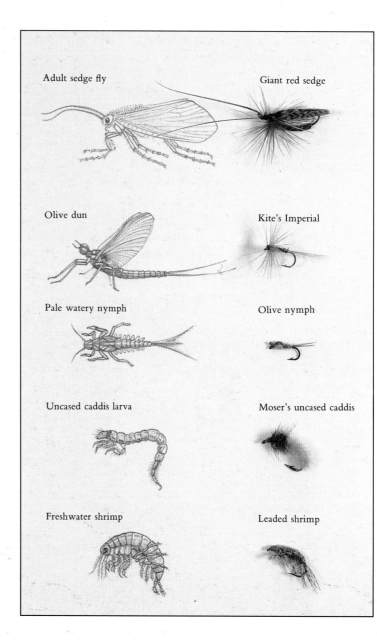

Adult sedge fly   Giant red sedge

Olive dun   Kite's Imperial

Pale watery nymph   Olive nymph

Uncased caddis larva   Moser's uncased caddis

Freshwater shrimp   Leaded shrimp

LEFT
River trout food – water flies – and the imitations used by anglers.

RIGHT
Hampshire's River Test – one of the world's most famous trout rivers. Chalkstreams like this, with a near-constant flow rate and abundance of food, provide ideal conditions for trout.

THE RIVER RAINBOW TROUT

The river rainbow trout, so prized for its glittering iridescent sheen, shares most of its home waters with its sea-run relative, the steelhead, and both are classified *Salmo gairdneri*. In most waters, the steelheads dominate the resident rainbows both in size and number. However, in some rivers around Crescent Lake in Washington State and the Kamloops Lakes of British Columbia, and in the Apache, Gila and McCloud Rivers of California, the migratory form has been lost because the trout of these waters are prevented from running to sea by physical barriers, such as dams.

The natural range of the wild rainbow trout extends from the Kuskokwim River region of Alaska to the Baja California Peninsula and the coastal rivers of Mexico. Within this region, many of the rivers draining into the Pacific still hold a head of resident wild rainbow trout, including the MacKenzie River of Oregon, the McCloud and Kern of California, Henry's Fork of the Snake River system in Idaho, the Babine River of British Columbia and the Kenai–Russia River system of Alaska. However, during the last 100 years, rainbow trout have been introduced into countless other waters throughout the world. Today, many rivers close to the original range in the USA and Canada have stocks of rainbow trout; but these are not native wild trout stocks.

In rivers that have both resident river rainbows and steelhead trout, it can be difficult to distinguish between the two. When the adult steelhead returns to the river from its feeding sojourn in the Pacific it is steel-grey or silvery in colour, but a flash of green, red and blue soon appears and the steelheads merge with the river rainbow trout. Most anglers solve the problem by calling the large trout of such a river steelheads, while the smaller fish are designated rainbows. This is probably fair enough, for no river can produce the quantity of food available in the ocean, and few if any river rainbows reach the average size of steelheads.

River rainbow trout spawn in the late winter or spring, at the same time as the migratory steelheads. We do not know whether they ever interbreed. Certainly they do not in the rivers of Washington State and British Columbia, which produce the biggest steelheads. There the gravel chosen by the steelheads when they cut their redds is too large for smaller rainbow trout, and often the flow in the reaches of the river used by the spawning steelheads is too strong for the smaller trout to mate. In other rivers they possibly do interbreed, for rainbow trout and steelheads have been reported on the same spawning gravel.

River rainbow trout are vigorous feeders. Unlike the river brown trout and cutthroat trout, which spend much of the non-breeding season in one lie and wait for the flow to bring food to them, the river rainbow will go in search of food. When there is little being carried by the stream, the trout will slowly cruise around a big pool or tack upstream, devouring anything that is edible. On one tiny feeder stream of the Alaskan Kenai, a feeding rainbow trout was observed covering almost a mile over a period of two hours.

The river rainbow also takes a much wider range of foods. After the fry stage, the brown trout and cutthroat ignore tiny morsels like algae and the smallest insect larvae and pupae. Rainbow trout will take these throughout their lives, and they also gather a much greater proportion of their food from the river bed: stonefly and mayfly nymphs

and caddis larvae. A short bout of feeding, either on bottom foods or on flies at the water surface, will satiate the brown and cutthroat trout, but not the rainbow.

As a result, river rainbows grow much faster than other trout in similarly productive waters. In rich English chalkstreams, brown trout reach between 12 and 14 inches in length only at three years of age. In the most productive rivers of Idaho and Montana, rainbow trout exceed these sizes at two years. One rainbow, caught from Jackson Hole, Wyoming, in 1976 scaled 6 lbs at just four years of age: yet this fish had been feeding mainly on the alga *Cladophora* and the tiniest of caddis larvae and stone fly nymphs.

With fast growth, rainbows reach sexual maturity earlier than cutthroats and brown trout. Rainbows tend to spawn first when they reach about 12–16 inches in length, often at the end of their second year. Brown trout and cutthroats may not mature until their third or fourth year. However, few wild rainbow trout survive more than two or three spawnings: their maximum life expectancy is about four or five years. River brown and cutthroat trout can reach eight, nine or even ten years.

ABOVE

The Yellowstone River is one of the few truly wild trout rivers that flow eastwards across the United States into the Atlantic.

Most wild trout rivers in North America drain into the Pacific.

the oxygen held by the water. And where the oxygen level falls to a certain point the river can no longer support trout.

The amount of oxygen contained in water is also affected by temperature. At $0°$ Centigrade, one litre of pure water can hold almost 15 milligrams of oxygen; but at $10°$ it can hold only 11 mg, and at $20°$ C less than 9 mg of oxygen. Yet the warmer the water, the more oxygen is needed by the trout. As a cold-blooded species, its body temperature rises with the temperature of the surrounding water—and the higher the temperature the more active the trout becomes, and the higher its oxygen demands. Hence its need for clean, cool water is absolute.

At very low water temperatures the trout is sluggish and needs little oxygen. When the water temperature is below $4°$C the trout will not feed: its energy level is too low. As the temperature rises the trout's activity and oxygen demands increase until a point is reached where the oxygen concentration in the water is no longer sufficient to produce the energy for feeding, growth and normal everyday metabolism. Many naturalists and anglers will have noted trout lying almost torpid in the flow during very hot summer weather when the temperature may reach $20°$C or more during the daytime. Warm weather will also increase the damage caused by organic wastes. The higher the temperature, the more active bacteria become, and thus the level of oxygen in the water falls further. During a prolonged heatwave, the trout may be forced to move either up- or downstream to cleaner water or to faster water, such as weir pools or shallow broken runs, where oxygen from the air is rapidly mixed in by the turbulence.

Where rivers flow through farmland, the water may be enriched by fertilizers (mainly nitrates and phosphates) leaching from the soil. This can enhance the growth of plants that are dangerous to trout. Where there is a very high concentration of phosphates an alga known as *Cladophora* or blanket-weed may flourish. As its common name suggests, *Cladophora* clothes the riverbed with a thick mat or blanket: a matted mass of slimy green fibres. During the day these plants produce oxygen in the process of photosynthesis, and in sunny weather the amount of oxygen they produce may result in the water becoming supersaturated with oxygen and the plants clothed with silver bubbles of gaseous oxygen. Come nightfall, however, the plants remove oxygen from the water and instead add carbon dioxide. During warm weather, the oxygen can fall to lethal levels, and the trout population will then have to move to rougher aerated reaches of the river or die.

The optimal water temperature for the incubation of trout eggs is between about $4°$ and $12°$C. Below this, the incubation period is prolonged: there is plenty of oxygen in the water, but the low temperature makes for only slow development. At higher temperatures more yolk is used for energy and less for growth, so the developing egg runs out of food before the fry has emerged. This is the reason why all trout—whether sea trout, lake trout or river trout—spawn in the coolest period of the year, and usually in the shallow, fast upper reaches of the river systems where the water is well oxygenated.

Even a river with clean, cool water, however, cannot support a thriving stock of wild trout unless the river bed provides the loose gravel in which the females cut redds and deposit their fertilized eggs. In Europe and North America, many streams have been damaged by canalisation or dredging, bridge-building or the laying of pipe-lines and cables, or the effects of riverside timber industry. Where these result in the silting up and concretion of the riverbed gravel, the trout find it difficult to cut redds. When eggs are deposited, they often fail to develop because the gravel surrounding them is clogged with

Barhaugh Burn

silt so that oxygenated water cannot percolate through.

A classic example of this is the Upper Avon, a very famous chalk-stream of southern England that was 'keepered by the late Frank Sawyer, doyen of the modern weighted nymph. From 1930 the river had been regularly stocked with fry, but in an article in *The Field* (April 1957) Sawyer described how, one evening in his cottage at Netheravon, he calculated what the natural stocks would be if the redds were in good order. 'The real answer to trout production,' he concluded, 'lies not in artificial hatching and fry-stocking, but in making the river do the work as intended by nature.' Sawyer went on to improve the redds mechanically and huge numbers of trout were produced by natural spawning in the river. Today, however, the river relies once more on artificial stocking, because it is expensive to keep the redds in good order.

Some of the great 19th century angler-naturalists emphasised that it was possible to distinguish the trout of one river system from those of a neighbouring river system, even where the waters were superficially identical. Today, it is hard to distinguish among river trout—whether brown, rainbow or cutthroat—on any basis other than size. This uniformity within each species is largely the result of artificial stocking, which has introduced non-native trout to most of the best fishing rivers of Europe and America.

Nonetheless, it seems certain that the Victorians were correct in their observations, for conditions vary so greatly from river to river that the native stocks must have adapted to their own particular niche. Differences in the geology and land use of the river catchment areas can make the flow rate and

mineral salt content of the water very different even in neighbouring rivers. One may produce more trout foods, or better gravel redds, than the other. Over the centuries, a different variety of trout will have evolved.

Most of the trout rivers of North America and Europe were originally colonised by fish moving upstream from the sea. When the last ice sheets retreated some 10,000 years ago, the sea-going forebears of today's brown, rainbow and cutthroat trout adopted the rivers as spawning grounds and nursery areas for their pre-smolt stages. As soon as the sea trout parr developed into smolts they would head off to sea. But eventually a proportion of the parr did not develop the smolt stage, and instead of migrating seawards they remained in the river. From these presumably emerged our resident river trout stocks.

The wild trout that spend their entire lives in rivers today are quite different in appearance, structure and behaviour from those first post-glacial colonisers. So rapidly do trout evolve genetically that, long before the 19th century naturalists began their investigations, generations of inbreeding in the rivers and adaptation to river life had resulted in a wide range of distinctive varieties of trout. Indeed it is likely that each wild trout river had produced a stock of trout specially adapted to its waters. Each river would impose different selective pressures on the newly-arrived stock, resulting eventually in slight differences of genetic composition in the resident trout.

However, since at least the beginning of the present century little regard has been given to the genetic qualities of a river's native trout stock. Where rivers suffer from over-fishing, or the native stock is considered too small either in population or in the average size of trout, artificial stocking has been widely carried out. In very few cases are rivers restocked with fish bred from the river's own strain. For this to happen, the organisation that controls the fishery must have its own hatchery and stew-ponds on the river. Ova and milt can then be obtained each year either from fish taken from the river or from a stock of native trout that are kept at the hatchery for that purpose. However, few fisheries have such facilities. Instead, commercial fish farms raise huge numbers of trout—brown, rainbow or cutthroat trout of no definite parentage—which are used to stock a wide range of different rivers.

In Europe, where fishing pressure is great, the variety of brown trout most commonly used to stock rivers is actually descended from a lake form, the Loch Leven trout. Even more remarkable is the introduction of foreign species of trout to supplement the stocks of the native wild trout. Many of the most famous brown trout rivers of Britain and Europe, including the hallowed River Test, are now heavily stocked each year with the American rainbow trout; and many rivers in the United States with a native cutthroat population have been artificially stocked with rainbow or brown trout.

The consequences of such haphazard artificial stocking are only now being considered by freshwater biologists, fish farmers and riverbank owners. As recently as July 1988, the Annual Scientific Meeting of the Freshwater Biological Association considered the whole issue. Dr J. M. Elliott, Director of the FBA, concluded that 'there was only one way to stock a river with trout satisfactorily, and that was to take the brood stock from the native fish in the river. Importing fish from fish-farms could lead to the whole population dying out.' (*Salmon, Trout and Sea Trout*, September 1988).

Where native trout stocks are sustained by raising brood stock in protected nurseries, the introduced fish will gradually be fished out. The wild trout population will reclaim its own waters, and the unique characteristics evolved over centuries may become apparent once more. But where heavy angling pressure creates the incentive to stock the river rapidly, regardless of cost, it may already be too late. What once were wild trout rivers are now merely stocked trout fisheries.

RIGHT
The Snake River, a tributary of the mighty Columbia River system. The headwaters, on the Wyoming-Idaho border, hold a variety of cutthroat considered by some scientists to be a separate form, carmichaeli. *The coastal cutthroat thrives in the lower reaches, together with the rainbow trout.*

THE RIVER CUTTHROAT TROUT

Most cutthroat systems have two separate populations of *Salmo clarki*, each with its own ecological niche. One inhabits the main river, the other resides in the smaller feeder streams and head waters. Those that inhabit the main river are much larger than the smaller stream residents: the main river usually produces more food and has a more constant environment in terms of temperature and flow, so it promotes a more rapid growth rate.

In the Columbia and Snake Rivers, for example, there are large numbers of four-year-old cutthroats measuring 16 inches and more, and weighing well in excess of the pound mark. In the high headwaters and feeder streams, small rough rocky streams set in pine forest and maple and alder woodland, the resident cutthroats at four years of age are often only six to eight inches in length and weigh in at three or four to the pound.

There is evidence that each of the populations within one river system remain separate, so the main river and the feeder streams may each be considered to have their own strain. When the main river cutthroat head upstream in the winter months to spawn during the spring in the smaller streams, they may spawn alongside the feeder stream trout. Often, however, the small-stream fish are separated by some barrier—a waterfall or dam—over which the big-river fish cannot pass, or the small-stream fish spawn a little later than those fish that have run upstream from the main river, or they spawn on different gravel beds. Soon after spawning, the trout from the main river tend to drop quickly downstream, and their fry often follow soon after emerging from the gravel redds. By contrast, the small-stream cutthroats tend to stay permanently close to their redds.

Many cutthroat river systems have been stocked with non-native trout, and the local strains have been lost. Where other forms of cutthroats have been introduced, they have interbred with the native cutthroats to produce a mongrel stock. Elsewhere, brown trout from Europe, or rainbow trout or brook trout (speckled char) from elsewhere in North America have ousted the native cutthroats from much of the river system. In some cases the introduced rainbows have hybridised with the native cutthroats, destroying the integrity of the local population.

Where the range of cutthroats overlaps naturally with the range of rainbow trout, the two may co-exist in the same river. Anglers fishing the big rivers of British Columbia, Washington State and Oregon often find that in the rough turbulent water at the neck of a pool the fly is taken by rainbow trout, while cutthroats are feeding a few yards downstream, where the flow slackens and the water deepens in the body of the pool. Where a rapid flow gushes through the centre of the pool, there may be rainbow trout; the cutthroats occupy the slow flow in a deep hole under the river bank.

Over the length of a river shared by wild stocks of cutthroats and rainbows, the rainbow trout often predominate in the lower reaches and the cutthroats upstream. So both species can find a separate niche; and where they do so they will not interbreed. Usually the cutthroats spawn earlier than the rainbows. And, possibly because they tend to be smaller than rainbow trout in the same river system, the cutthroats move higher up the feeder streams and cut their redds in smaller gravel than the rainbow trout.

RIGHT

The West Slope cutthroat (sometimes called the Montana Blackspot) has a heavily speckled tail and characteristic red slashes on the throat. River cutthroat tend to be much smaller than river rainbow trout.

Study/pencil and wash

However, problems arise when rainbow trout are put into rivers which were formerly occupied only by cutthroats. In such waters, the main-river cutthroats will have taken the faster water lies that provide more food, while the smaller ones hold lies in the less productive feeder streams. When rainbow trout are introduced they compete with the cutthroats throughout the river, taking the prime lies from the bigger fish and devouring the smaller cutthroats. They will use any redd gravel to spawn, either interbreeding with the cutthroats or interfering with their breeding cycle by ousting the cutthroats from the better gravel and devouring their ova and fry.

COLORADO CUTTHROAT *Salmo clarki pleuriticus*

RIO GRANDE CUTTHROAT *Salmo clarki virginalis*

ABOVE

These two diminutive varieties of river cutthroat trout are largely restricted to the headwaters of the Colorado and Rio Grande river systems in the southwest of the United States. In their pure native form, they are found only in waters that introduced varieties of trout cannot reach.

CHAPTER THREE
WILD TROUT IN LAKES

An immense variety of lakes are inhabited by wild trout. On the cols of the highest mountains they live in small rocky tarns, or deep pools filling the ice-gouged floors of high level corries. Lower down the slopes are valley lakes, long, narrow, deep and—as the valley meanders—sinuous. These were carved out by the ice sheets that once covered much of the wild trout's geographical range. When the glaciers retreated, great piles of rubble known as morraine were left blocking the entrances to these valleys: natural dams behind which water was retained.

Where there are flat peaty moorlands, as over much of Canada, the northwestern United States, Lapland and northwestern Britain, lakes have formed in hollows set in rock outcrops and depressions in the peat. In such countryside, a complex of lakes may occupy a greater area than the dry land. Close to Achmore on the Isle of Lewis in the Outer Hebrides you can see thirteen such pools at once, all within a mile or so, without moving your head, and you can catch wild brown trout in each of them. Close to the Finnish town of Rovaniemi the lakes and pools are so numerous that it would be impossible to visit them all in one summer month.

By contrast, the lakes found in the Irish plain are set on major river systems, in shallow rock and peat hollows. These lakes are nowhere of great depth, but may be large in area and broken up by inlets and bays and a scattering of islands and skerries. Lough Corrib, in County Galway, is reputed to have 365 such islands—one for every day of the year. But if two people count them independently the figures they arrive at are always different.

With so much variety among lakes, it is not surprising that the fish themselves vary tremendously. This is the result of several interacting factors: the quality of the lake water and its plant nutrients, which determine the nature and quantity of the trout food; the presence or otherwise of food species such as large crustaceans and small forage fish; the ecological niches within the lake and the behaviour of the trout in these niches; and the genetic composition of the trout. In broad terms, variation among lake trout is determined by the available food supplies and the genes of the trout themselves.

Unlike river trout, which obtain the bulk of their food from the flow at or close to the water surface, lake trout must swim in search of their food. Only a small proportion is gathered at the surface. The vast majority of lake trout seek out the more productive shallow water at the lake margins or amongst skerries and islands in the lake. Here they are likely to find the most plant growth and the water animals that feed off the plants. Some lakes produce large numbers of crustaceans, such as freshwater shrimps, hog-lice and crayfish. Such a diet provides a high level of carotenoids—the orange-red pigment found in crustaceans—and promotes the brightest coloured trout, with vivid red or pink markings on the fins and scales and a 'salmon-pink' flesh colour. Where there is little in the way of crustacean food, the diet is dominated by insect-life or small forage fishes and the trout tend to be drabber: reds and pinks are fainter and the flesh is usually white or pale grey.

In larger lakes it is possible to find trout in several different niches, often with different coloration. Some of the trout might patrol areas of weedbed or shallow rocky shores, where aquatic snails and crustaceans are abundant. These fish will tend to be brighter in colour than trout that lie in the mouth of inflowing streams and feed mainly on aquatic insects: other trout in the same lake may feed almost entirely on other fish. These will tend to have the plainest coloration of all.

So, although it may be possible to identify a lake trout

purely on the basis of colour, an individual gillaroo, Kamloops rainbow or Yellowstone cutthroat may well be different in general coloration from others in the same lake. Some gillaroos are much less red than others; some Kamloops trout have much brighter pink scales and fins than others; some Yellowstone cutthroats are a much darker brown than others. Yet despite this variation it is usually possible to recognize a particular variety because the underlying features are always present.

The behaviour of trout in lakes is directly linked to feeding. Some trout, including lake rainbow trout and sonaghens, feed predominantly on zooplankton in the open deep water, especially in summer. Since these zooplankton often occur in localized high concentrations, the lake trout tend to shoal, since a large group of trout hunting together are more likely to find such food than an individual fish. By contrast some of the predatory, fish-eating trout tend to be solitary; a shoal of small forage-fish are more easily stalked by an individual than by a shoal. The majority of trout concentrate on taking a wide range of invertebrate foods from the shallow lake margins. They form loose associations or shoals and cruise over vast areas in search of their insect, mollusc and crustacean foods. However, some margin-feeders, notably the gillaroo, are more specialized: they occupy small areas of the lake bed, which they scour for food rather like a river trout in its lie.

Most lake trout, however, will change their behaviour during the year, or even from day to day. In early spring, when zooplankton is scarce, all the trout may be concentrated around the lake margins. As the zooplankton populations build up in late spring many trout will leave the margins for the deep water plankton clouds. Then, as autumn rains cool the lake and the zooplankton stocks decline, the deep-water trout move back either to the margins or to the mouths of feeder streams. Even in

mid-summer a shoal of trout that are feeding on zooplankton, many feet below the surface, may change behaviour and diet rapidly. An evening fall of insects on to the water surface will cause them to rise; or torrential rain may result in a spate of the feeder streams, so the trout will move there to gather food carried by the floodwater and, as they do, they take up lies like river trout.

ABOVE
Lough Corrib, in County Galway, is one of Ireland's most prolific lakes. A huge population of trout thrive in the rich waters, reaching a large average size.

LEFT
Malham Tarn, the source of Yorkshire's River Aire, is set amidst spectacular limestone scenery. Trout grow quickly in the lake waters, which are high in nutrients.

The size of trout varies enormously from one lake to another. This is clearly seen in the table below, which gives measurements of fish from lakes in the British Isles. The fish were measured from tip of the snout to the fork in the tail (using scale readings):

AVERAGE LENGTH OF LAKE BROWN TROUT AT THREE YEARS

Lake	Ins	Cms
Lough Derravaragh (Co. Westmeath)	13.0	32.7
Loch Lanlish (Sutherland)	12.8	32.0
Loch Caladail (Sutherland)	12.1	30.3
Lough Corrib (Co. Galway)	11.9	29.7
Lough Mask (Co. Mayo)	11.7	29.3
Malham Tarn (Yorkshire)	11.4	28.5
Windermere (Cumbria)	8.5	21.3
Loch Lomond (Argyll)	7.9	19.9
Loch Fadagoa (Lewis)	6.8	17.1
Loch Urrahag (Lewis)	6.6	16.2
Wastwater (Cumbria)	6.1	15.2
Red Tarn (Cumbria)	4.6	11.5

(Data from Malcolm Greenhalgh, *Lake, Loch & Reservoir Trout Fishing*, 1987)

Such measurements give a clear indication of the productivity of each lake: it is clear that Red Tarn, a high level corrie in the English Lake District, is very unproductive, while Loch Lanlish and Lough Derravaragh are highly productive. But why should some lakes produce fast-growing wild trout?

Latitude, which is sometimes held to be an influence, evidently has little effect. The highly productive lochs of Sutherland are in the far north of Scotland; while Malham Tarn,

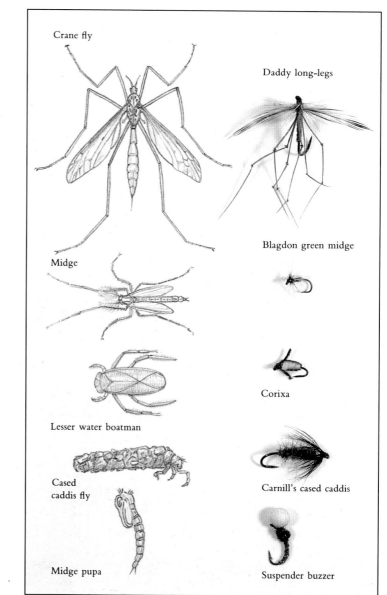

Crane fly

Daddy long-legs

Midge

Blagdon green midge

Lesser water boatman

Corixa

Cased caddis fly

Carnill's cased caddis

Midge pupa

Suspender buzzer

LEFT
Lake trout foods – water flies and shrimps – and the imitations used by anglers.

RIGHT
A Loch Leven trout, cruising in midsummer, snatches midges from the surface as they hatch.

Pastel

THE LAKE BROWN TROUT

A bag of a dozen brown trout from one lake—whether it be a peaty lochan in the Hebrides, a deep rocky loch from the Scottish highlands, a Cumbrian lake such as Windermere, an Irish lough or a Swedish tarn—will often exhibit an exhilarating range of colour. Some may be dark, almost black, with hardly any red or black spots. Others appear as if fresh-run from the sea: silver with small black spots. Between the two extremes is the characteristic brownie with dark brown back, golden yellow belly, red adipose fin, bright red spots and black speckles; one of the most beautiful of fish.

Where such variation occurs in one lake the fish have possibly been taken from different niches within the lake. The darkest, almost black, trout are usually found in holes close to the bank: perhaps where inflowing streams enter the lake through deep-cut peaty beds. Those that inhabit sandy-bottomed areas of shallow water often exhibit a pale sandy brown coloration. Those with the more typical brown trout colour are usually taken from the weedy lake margins. And the lighter silvery trout are often caught in deep water, where they feed on animal plankton.

The fish are camouflaged in their niches, and their coloration can change if the trout settle into a different background. It appears that trout can alter their pigmentation through a mechanism that works through the nervous and endocrine systems, triggered by light playing on the eyes. Trout that live in underground streams where there is no light at all, as in the limestone caves and potholes of the Yorkshire Dales and Alps, are usually colourless. However, blind fish are always dark in colour and this probably accounts for the mention, in many angling texts, of horrid, old black trout that refused to rise to the surface fly.

Diet as well as habitat influences the trout's coloration, especially in determining the extent and intensity of the colours red and orange. Fish caught in deep water, with bold red spotting and pink flesh, are presumably feeding on tiny planktonic crustaceans like *Daphnia*. If caught in the shallow margins they are probably feeding on freshwater shrimps. Such crustaceans, which have massive amounts of the orange pigment carotein in their tissues, provide much of the red pigment in wild brown trout. Trout that never eat crustaceans have subdued red spots and pale flesh.

There are almost certainly more wild brown trout living in lakes than in rivers, where they often face competition from introduced trout. But nearly all brown trout spend some of their lives in rivers, for most lake trout spawn in the rivers entering or draining the lake. They begin their move towards the spawning streams in September, when the autumn rainfall swells the river flow. At this time quite huge concentrations can be found near the mouths of inflowing streams. The shoals move upstream to spawn, usually during November or December. The lake trout and river trout often share the same spawning areas, but it is not known whether lake and river trout interbreed. If they do, then we must consider that the river and lake brown trout are of the same stock.

The adults return downstream, but it is unusual to find brown trout parr in a lake, which suggests that the young trout do not enter the lake until they are at least two years old. This is borne out from observations on the smallest of lakes, where the feeder streams are mere trickles. These tiny

LEFT
Scotland's Loch Ness is very deep. The brown trout it produces are generally small, but some become large ferox trout, eating smaller fish and living to a great age.

feeder streams may be crammed with small brown trout parr, but where the water deepens as the stream enters the lake the parr are absent. Possibly the deep stillwater of the lake is too dangerous a place for small trout parr. There are often more predators there: divers (loons) and grebes, goosanders and mergansers, perch and pike, even large trout. In the deep open water of a lake the parr may be far more vulnerable.

So as fry and parr, lake trout live side by side with river trout. We do not know why some parr eventually move to the lake while others remain in the river. Is it by conditioning or by genetics, by chance or by choice? Do some brown trout become lake trout one year and river trout the next? Although scientists have been studying wild brown trout for a century and more, and anglers have watched their habits for hundreds of years, many questions still remain unanswered.

set in the Yorkshire Moors, is one of the most southerly natural trout lakes in Britain and also produces sizeable fish. In North America, some Alaskan lakes produce larger trout than lakes in the central Rockies; and in continental Europe some Alpine lakes produce smaller trout than lakes in the subarctic regions of Norway and Sweden.

Another common theory is that the fewer trout a lake contains, the larger on average they will be: the inference being that fewer trout means more food per fish and therefore more growth. So strongly has this belief been held that anglers have introduced predatory pike into some trout lakes in an attempt to thin out the tiny fish so that those that remain have more food and will grow bigger. Elsewhere trout have been netted out in the hope that those that remain will grow larger.

These efforts have largely proved futile, because in reality the trout that are left cannot take all the food that would have been taken by those that were weeded out. In such lakes the food is so sparse that the energy expended in seeking the extra food offsets the gain: the trout may eat more, but they do not convert the extra to flesh. They were on a subsistence diet before the cull; after the cull the remainder still do not have enough food readily available for rapid growth. In any case, as soon as the remaining fish breed, the stock is replaced by more small fish. The problem is simply that the lake does not produce enough food for fast growth, no matter how many trout are in the lake.

Others have argued that the trout in some lakes are genetically adapted for more rapid growth. There is some evidence for this: the Pyramid Lake variety of cutthroat was large; but other strains introduced into Pyramid Lake never attained such size, perhaps because they lacked a gene for rapid growth. Elsewhere, the results have often been different. Tiny wild brown trout have been netted from some lakes where the food production is low and the trout correspondingly small, and put into nearby lakes where the productivity is high. The result: the tiny stunted trout suddenly begin to grow rapidly. So the growth rate, and thus size, of wild trout in a lake probably depends mainly on the amount of food produced by the lake.

To understand why one lake produces more food and bigger trout than another, we must examine the food chain, or food web, in those waters. At the base of the chain, as with all food production, are the green plants which feed the herbivores, which in turn are eaten by the carnivores in the lake. The trout itself is a carnivore, feeding mainly on lesser herbivorous animals in the water such as midge larvae, water snails, mayfly nymphs and many other creatures. The more herbivores in the water, the faster the growth of the trout. But the herbivores in turn rely on the plant life of the lake for their food. Thus the more plant life in a lake, the more food for the herbivores and the more herbivores for the trout. The key to a productive trout lake is its ability to produce lush plant life.

As most gardeners know, plant production depends on several factors: water, sunlight, carbon dioxide gas from the atmosphere, and mineral salts (fertilizers) which the plants combine in their green tissues to produce growth. The amount of water in a lake is usually abundant, although some lakes can dry up. In lakes used as reservoirs, excessive water removal during a dry summer may result in the lake margins drying out, with the loss of marginal vegetation and invertebrate trout foods. But the amount of sunlight striking a lake, and the concentration of carbon dioxide in the air and dissolved in water remain fairly constant in any particular region.

ABOVE
*A three-year-old Loch
Leven trout shows the
apricot fins and delicately
tinted scales characteristic of
the smaller Leven trout.*

Field study/pencil and wash

Consequently, it is likely that the greatest variation from one lake to the next will be in the concentration of mineral salts: the fertilizers that stimulate plant growth. These minerals enter the water from the soil of the catchment area, leached out by rain percolating through the soil and washed via feeder streams into the lake. Where the lake is set in a catchment area of shallow soil, acid peat or hard rock that is resistant to weathering, the amount of mineral salts picked up by the water draining into the lake will be tiny. However, where the lake has a catchment area set in the midst of deep rich soil, or where the underlying rock readily releases its mineral salts into the water, the lake will have a high concentration of salts. The more salts the more plant growth; the more plant growth, the more herbivores and the faster-growing will be the trout.

The variation is most striking where productive lakes occur only a short distance from unproductive lakes. In the islands of the Outer Hebrides, off the coast of northwest Scotland, the west coastal plain is buffeted by Atlantic gales that carry huge amounts of white shell-sand up to three miles inland to produce 'machair', a florally rich coastal strip nurtured by the salt-rich sand. There are many small lochs in the machair, where the growth of aquatic plant life is rich. And in these lochan, the brown trout grow big: a two-pounder is quite common. Only a few miles inland, however, the influence of the mineral-rich sand is lost. In the peaty lochan here the weed growth is much less and a half-pound trout considered to be a good one.

A similar case occurs in Sutherland on the nutrient-rich limestone of the Durness Peninsula. On Loch Lanlish all fish under 2 lbs must be returned and on neighbouring lochs the fish average close on that size. By contrast, in the nearby hills, where the nutrient-rich limestone is replaced by hard, resistant granites and gneiss, there are lochs where it would take a bag of ten fish

RIGHT
A small ferox trout from Lough Melvin. In appearance it is close to a brown trout, but structural features such as the huge mouth and powerful jaws are clearly present.

Field study/pastel

to push the scale down to the 2 lb mark. In the Kamloops region of British Columbia, some lakes produce native rainbow trout that grow to 50 lbs or more. Other lakes that formerly had no Kamloops trout were stocked with the same variety, but in these lakes the trout rarely reached 5 lbs in weight. Again it is a matter of productivity of the lake water: the higher, stocked lakes have a less nutrient-rich water supply than the lower Kamloops lakes.

Another factor influencing the production of trout food in lakes is the depth of the water. Sunlight will be blocked out beyond a certain depth, so if the water is too deep the lake bed will be in permanent darkness and plants will not be able to grow there, even if the silt on the bottom is rich in plant nutrients. However, plant life in the form of microscopic plant plankton can still grow in the illuminated surface layer of deep water. Feeding on these will be animal plankton such as the

water flea *Daphnia* and the larvae of phantom-flies *Chaoborus*, on which trout will feed. The more nutrient salts in the water, the greater the growth of plant and animal plankton and, of course, trout.

Where the water is rich in plant nutrients and the lake is so shallow that sunlight can reach to the lake bed there will be lush growths of rooted weeds on the bottom as well as huge quantities of plankton drifting in the water. Such waters have the fastest trout growth. Where the water has very small concentrations of nutrients and the lake bed falls away steeply so that only a narrow margin of lake bed receives sunlight, there will be relatively tiny amounts of plankton and a very sparse growth of rooted water weed in the illuminated margins. These waters have the slowest trout growth.

Freshwater biologists divide lakes into three categories according to their productivity. Those whose water contains very little in the way of mineral salts are described as *oligotrophic*. Often the water is so clean that it can be drunk by humans with the minimum of treatment. Such lakes have little plant growth, sparse populations of invertebrate animals, and a head of tiny trout. Lakes with fair concentrations of mineral salts that can support a good growth of plants are termed *mesotrophic*. The invertebrate populations are diverse and abundant, and the head of trout large. Such waters are considered the best trout lakes.

The third category is *eutrophic* lakes with very high concentrations of mineral salts. Usually a large proportion of these salts originates from human activities—the leaching of farm fertilizers into the lake, the piping of sewage and organic industrial effluent from lakeside towns, the washings from dairy farms. When these accumulate in the lake water, they result in massive growths of plant material, including large blooms of planktonic algae that can make the water a characteristic olive or green colour. Bacterial activity in such waters is often high. The bacteria feed either on dead plant matter or on untreated sewage or industrial waste that has been piped into the lake. This can make the oxygen level in the lake water very low, especially when the water is warm in summer. Some marginally eutrophic lakes can support populations of very large trout. Should over-eutrophication occur, its effect will be the death of the fish, including trout, in the lake.

Fortunately, most wild trout lakes are not surrounded by intensively-farmed land, or situated close to large towns and cities. However, Ireland's largest lake, Lough Neagh, has suffered greatly through over-eutrophication with massive algal blooms, increased bacterial action and the death of huge

Caudal:
Much Fin damage

Lower fin darker
and extremeties of
all rays smudged black.
Fin damage.

Ends of rays smudged black
Darker and more so toward
Fore-edge - some damage

LEFT

*A silvery ferox trout,
hunting alone, ambushes a
shoal of char in a Scottish
loch.*

Pastel and wash

ABOVE

*A ferox trout, showing the
long, flattened head shape
and powerful jaws
characteristic of this
variety; the fin damage is
also common in large fish.*

*Although some ferox trout
are silver-hued, others are
a very dark brown with a
few black spots.*

Field study/pencil

THE SONAGHEN TROUT

Early scientists called the sonaghen *Salmo nigripinnis*, after one of its most distinctive features. The Latin name—*nigri*, black; *pinnis*, fins—is a direct translation of its alternative common name, the black-finned trout. Today the variety is found only in Ireland's Lough Melvin, but at one time, it was also believed to occur in some Welsh mountain lakes, where it was referred to as the Welsh black-finned trout.

Dr Günter, the 19th century fish biologist, gave Llyn Beguilin in Merionethshire and Llyn Gadr on the slopes of Cader Idris as two such lakes that were inhabited by this form. However, it seems that these Welsh fish are highly variable and are better considered ordinary lake brown trout that, because of the nature of their habitat, have a dark pigmentation.

The sonaghen is a quite distinct trout in both appearance and behaviour. It is a relatively small fish, averaging less than ten inches in length and well under a pound in weight. In colour it is superficially very plain: steel-blue, darker on the back, with a few distinct black spots and a very few dull red or orange ones. The black fins are eye-catching for they are not simply dark or blackish, they are truly black. Two other features of the sonaghen that a close examination reveals are a relatively large head and mouth, and a very large caudal (or tail) fin. These give us a clue as to the lake life of the fish.

Sonaghen differ from other forms of brown trout in that they spend their entire lives, outside the spawning period, in very deep water. In the depths of the lough they feed on shoals of zooplankton: tiny crustaceans that in turn feed on immense clouds of microscopic plant plankton. The shoals of zooplankton drift around the lake, so the sonaghen must follow them. And because their prey is so tiny they do not pick them off individually. Instead they swim along, with mouths open, filtering them from the water by the thousand. Hence they have evolved a large mouth as a water-strainer and a large caudal fin to propel them on their meanderings around the lough.

There are periods of the year when the populations of zooplankton are too small to sustain the sonaghen, notably from autumn through to late spring. Then they will feed on insects that have been blown on to the lake or drifted from the shallow margins into the deeps. But, save for the brief spawning season in early winter, they appear not to leave the deep water. That is their niche, and they stick to it. Even though they share Lough Melvin with the gillaroo, the two forms rarely meet, for they are ecological opposites.

It is thought that the ancestor of the sonaghen was a sea-going trout that colonised the lake, via the Drowes River, from the Atlantic following the retreat of the arctic ice some 10,000 years ago. This colonisation was separate from those of other sea-going trout which gave rise to the gillaroo, ferox and Atlantic sea trout that also are still present in the lough. As a Queen's University of Belfast study has shown, each of these has remained genetically isolated; and each has its own niche in the lough system.

RIGHT

A sonaghen trout from Lough Melvin. The proportionally large tail fin and streamlined figure enable the sonaghen to compete within the feeding shoal.

Specimen study/watercolour

SONAGHEN BROWN TROUT
Salmo trutta trutta

THE FEROX TROUT

To some naturalists a ferox or great lake trout is simply a large brown trout that feeds primarily on fish. To others it is a species of trout in its own right, the *Salmo ferox*. But all agree on the main characteristics of the ferox: a big wild trout that is found in natural lakes in Europe; with a big head and grotesquely long, broad powerful jaws that bear some resemblance to the pike's; a fairly plain silvery or dull brown coloration, possibly with a greenish or olive hue; a fish-eater. To these physical features we must add one other ferox characteristic: great longevity.

Most of the British and Irish lakes that appear to hold ferox trout tend to be fairly unproductive: lakes like Lochs Morar, Ness, Arkaig, Awe and Quoich in Scotland, Ullswater and Bassenthwaite in Cumbria, Loughs Eask and Melvin in Ireland and Llyns Padarn and Peris set amidst the mountains of Snowdonia. In these waters a typical brown trout caught on rod and line will be less than a pound in weight and between three and five years of age. But very occasionally the angling press will announce the capture of a trout weighing up to ten pounds or more.

There is considerable evidence that the number of big ferox trout has declined during this century. In the 1800s they were not uncommon, but a wild ten-pounder is now a rarity. This may be related to the decline of the Atlantic salmon and sea trout, on which the ferox feed. Most ferox lakes have adults of these species passing through them to spawn in the lakes' feeder streams. After spawning, the much-weakened kelts drop back to the lakes; and two or three years later the sea-going smolts pass through the lake on their way to the sea. These are the ferox's prey; and the great reduction in numbers of these rich sources of food has presumably contributed to the scarceness of big ferox.

In a study of Lough Melvin, biologists from the Queen's University, Belfast showed that the ferox trout is genetically different from the other forms of trout that inhabit that lake. They spawn with other ferox trout in separate streams from the other trout that live there. Furthermore, Andrew Ferguson and his co-workers showed that it is possible to identify, by genetic finger-printing, tiny ferox trout that may superficially resemble ordinary brown trout. On these grounds Ferguson argued, in the *Went Memorial Lecture* given to the Royal Dublin Society on 20 November 1985, that the ferox in Melvin were a full species in their own right that had evolved from a single colonisation of the lough following the last Ice Age.

As yet, we have no similar studies from other ferox lakes, so the biological identity of the ferox remains a puzzle. If ferox are merely overgrown carnivorous trout, why do some trout become fish-eaters and grow to great age and size while the vast majority do not? But if ferox are members of a separate species, why are there no records in the angling literature of small ferox trout?

Only the most tentative conclusions can be drawn at present. Briefly, within the brown trout stocks of some lakes are genes which confer on their possessors the ability to grow to great age and to great size, and a behavioural trait to turn almost exclusively to a diet of fish once they have reached a certain size. Other trout, the majority, do not have these genes; they have a much shorter lifespan and although like all trout they will feed keenly on very small fish fry at times, they will not change their feeding pattern to concentrate on hunting fish.

RIGHT
A ferox trout. This Irish specimen scaled 11 lb 11 oz and was ten years old when caught. Few other trout in European lakes grow to anything like this size.

Measured drawing/pencil and wash

THE GILLAROO TROUT

'On a background of satin wood are scattered spots and blotches of red, orange, umber, and burnt sienna, so thickly as to touch and interfuse,' enthused T. C. Kingsmill Moore in *A Man May Fish* (1960). As the fish comes to the net, the impression can be well-nigh dazzling. To appreciate the richness of colour and complexity of patterning a quick look is not enough. You sit there in the boat, examining every spot, every line. Seeing how one shade merges into another. Poring over the fin markings. Scrutinising the subtle way that each individual scale contributes to the immaculate beauty of the whole.

The status of this highly distinctive fish has been the subject of argument for many years. Some have considered it to be a separate species: Günter gave the gillaroo the scientific name *Salmo stomachicus* because of its supposedly specific stomach structure. As the Reverend Houghton put it in 1879, in *British Fresh-Water Fishes*, 'The muscular walls of the Gillaroo are so strong that they have been supposed to perform to a certain extent the function of a gizzard.'

The gillaroo has evolved this feature as an adaptation to its diet: mainly invertebrates of the lake bed, including a high proportion of freshwater snails and crustaceans. The thick muscular wall is used to grind up these very tough food items. However, many other forms of trout can develop a similar thickened stomach wall when feeding for a long period on similar foods. So it is no more unique as a characteristic than the intense red colour of the gillaroo's flesh, caused by a high level of carotenoids in the diet.

There has been much debate as to whether the coloration of the gillaroo is primarily genetic or a product of the trout's diet and environment. A Queen's University of Belfast study of Lough Melvin has shown, for that lake at least, that the gillaroo is genetically isolated from the lake's other trout inhabitants, and that the progeny of gillaroos are always gillaroos. But no similar analysis of gillaroos from other lakes has been carried out.

However, a visual examination of gillaroos from Lough Conn and seven lochs in northwest Scotland has suggested that they may be closely related. Certainly, it would be very difficult to separate, on superficial characteristics alone, the gillaroos of Loughs Conn and Corrib, or Lochs Fadagoa, Mulach-Corrie and Assynt, either from each other or from those of Lough Melvin. Possibly they are all the progeny of one wave of trout that colonised the west of the British Isles from the Atlantic up to 10,000 years ago; and which because of their diet and behaviour have remained separate from other trout stocks ever since.

The gillaroo is generally a shallow water species, feeding close to the lake margins, around skerries and over rocky shelves, often in no more than a foot or so of water. In such niches it is well camouflaged despite its gaudiness: the bright patterning of the gillaroo merges into the flickering of sunlight on the boulder-strewn lake bed. Here the gillaroo browse the surface of rock and weed for snails, freshwater shrimps and hog-lice. They sift through the silt on the lake bed for caddisfly larvae, eating them case and all. Should there be a hatch of mayfly, or a fall of heather flies, they are not averse to rising the short distance to the surface to take them with a swirl.

RIGHT
A gillaroo: the gaudy Irish 'red feller' is one of the most spectacular brown trout varieties. Its brassy coloration provides camouflage against rocks and boulders in the shallow waters of lake margins.

Specimen study/watercolour

GILLAROO BROWN TROUT
Salmo trutta trutta

LEFT
Crescent Lake, in the Olympic National Park, Washington State, has two species of wild trout – the Beardslee rainbow and a lake form of the coastal cutthroat that is also known as the speckled trout.

numbers of fish, including trout and even the fairly pollution-tolerant Atlantic eel. Further south, in the Irish Republic, two famous and highly productive trout lakes (Loughs Sheelin and Derravaragh) are now close to over-eutrophication because of the effects of high nitrate and phosphate levels from the leaching of farm fertilizers. In Scotland there have been the first signs of the same problem on Loch Leven, the most famous trout lake in the world.

Lakes close to urban areas have been damaged, often unwittingly, in a number of other ways, with serious effects on the wild trout stocks. Many trout lakes have been exploited for reservoirs, which has often involved constructing a dam across the outflowing river. This can mean that the trout in the lake are cut off from an important breeding area. Most lake trout do not spawn in the lake. To breed they move into the feeder streams or outflowing river so that they can cut their redds in gravel, through which there will be a continuous flow of oxygenated water. Where trout do spawn in the lake they invariably do so on gravel banks close to an inflowing or outflowing stream. If the trout are cut off from the outflow and the feeder streams cannot provide enough extra redds, then the population of trout in that lake may decline.

Overfishing is another threat to trout stocks. Lakes often seem vast, with an infinite supply of fish. So, while river fishing is often controlled by bag limits, catch-and-release rules or restrictions on angling methods to protect the fish stocks, lake fishing is frequently uncontrolled. The consequence is that some lakes, especially in populous regions, suffer badly from overfishing. In larger lakes, trout stocks may suffer from commercial exploitation: Pyramid Lake in Nevada has lost its special variety of cutthroat trout partly as a result of overfishing with nets.

The local authority's solution to such problems is almost always to stock the water artificially with trout from a fish farm. If this is done with the same variety of trout that is native to the lake then no harm is done. However, this is rarely the case. It is not unusual for overfished lakes to be stocked with an entirely different species of trout, or even with artificially produced hybrid or sterile triploid trout.

Such approaches to boosting the head of trout in a lake are very short-sighted. Just as every river system has evolved its own variety of trout, the same is true of lakes. In fact the distinctive features of the wild trout in some lakes are so marked that many varieties have in the past been considered distinct species of trout. Many lakes have trout stocks that have been isolated from other trout for several thousand years. They have become genetically adapted to life in the lake. To risk exterminating these varieties by introducing alien stocks is nothing less than ecological vandalism, upsetting the biological structure of the lake and obliterating the results of thousands of years of evolution by the wild trout.

Pollution in lakes affects both native and introduced trout, and in the long term the effects are far more damaging than in rivers because the through-flow is extremely slow. It has been calculated that it takes 360 days, or almost a year, for all the water in a lake like Windermere, in the English Lake District, to pass through the outflowing river and be replaced by water from the feeder streams. In larger lakes such as Yellowstone it might take several years for all the water to flow through. So, while a 'one-off' pollution incident in a river may have been completely washed away within a couple of days, in a lake it may take months or even years.

However, the effects of pollution are noticed more slowly than in rivers. In lakes, the volume of water can be immense, and pollution accumulates insidiously before its effects are observed. This is most strikingly illustrated in cases of acidification: pollution by rain carrying high concentrations of substances such as sulphuric acid that originate from industrial gaseous emissions. In rivers the effect is immediate. In June 1980 a heavy acid rainfall almost wiped out the fish stocks of the Cumbrian Esk overnight. But by dropping alkaline chalk into the feeder streams, acid rain can be neutralised, allowing the fish stocks to recover. In lakes the effects are much less rapid. The pollutants build up slowly in the vast volume of water, and it can be difficult to prove that a particular incident of pollution has, in fact, occurred.

Nonetheless, over large areas of southern Scandinavia and northern Britain and some parts of the USA and Canada close to large centres of industry, the disastrous effects of acidification on lakes and their wild trout stocks have been clearly established. In these regions an increasing number of lakes are found to have reduced trout stocks, or trout that exhibit damage caused by high acid levels. Some lakes, that formerly had thriving stocks of wild trout, have even been reported as being dead lakes, entirely bereft of fish.

The Report of the Palaeoecology Research Unit (May 1988), *Lake Acidification in the United Kingdom*, prepared for Britain's Department of the Environment, identified the signs and effects of acidification in some British lakes in west Wales, northwest England, southwest Scotland and the Scottish highlands, where concern had been expressed on the deterioration of the water and its fish stocks. The unit noted a

five to fifteenfold increase of acidity since 1850, and the contamination of some lakes since about 1800 by industrially-derived air pollutants including trace metals, soot and fly-ash.

The effects on the fish stocks of this pollution are quite horrific. The fishery at Scotland's Loch Laidon, well known for its brown and ferox trout, is reported to have declined. The trout stocks through much of Galloway in southwest Scotland have been decimated; some waters are fishless. Llyn y Bi in Wales, which had up to 1930 a good head of char and brown trout, is 'now virtually fishless'.

As agriculture and industry continue to intensify, old towns grow and new towns are built, the threat to lakes from eutrophication, overfishing and pollution is likely to increase. Lakes that are in danger at present may lose their wild trout, and even some of those that are currently not at risk may suffer. It will take great courage on the part of politicians to reverse this trend. But there is a ray of hope: environmental issues are worth votes today.

Both in North America and in Europe there are signs of a growing political will to enforce the reduction of agricultural pollution and the emission of industrial gases into the atmosphere. Indeed reports suggest that the condition of some lakes is improving subsequent to the reduction of pollution; and in some lakes the acidity has been reduced by liming. However, urgent action is necessary to protect individual trout varieties. Where native trout are lost, the new stock can only come from the fish-farm, and this means fish of possibly unknown origin taking over the lakes.

RIGHT
A Crescent Lake, or Beardslee, rainbow.

Pastel and wash

THE KAMLOOPS LAKES TROUT

In 1812 the first white settlers of the western foothills of the Rockies and the plains and valleys of inland British Columbia established a fort settlement which they called Fort Kamloops. A few years later a nearby lake on the Thompson River was given the same name, Lake Kamloops. From this lake, and also from others in the same area—including Adams, Kootenay and Shuswap—the early settlers caught large numbers of big silver trout.

So prolific were these fisheries that towards the end of the 19th century the Kamloops began to attract numbers of visiting anglers. In 1892 two visitors sent some specimen trout to Professor D. S. Jordan who gave the fish the name *Salmo kamloopsii*. This was during the days of the 'species splitters': today the trout of the Kamloops lakes are regarded as a variety of the rainbow trout *Salmo gairdneri*.

The Kamloops lakes are set in the midst of hills that rise to 6,000 feet. The valley floors are often too dry and windswept to support forest. Grassland and sage scrub predominate, though in marshy hollows and at the water's edge there are stands of willow, aspen and cottonwood. Stretching beyond is the forest, with fir, pine and larch at lower levels, and lodgepole pine and spruce on the higher slopes. The wooded hillsides retain water, providing a regular flow to the feeder streams in which the trout spawn. As the water slowly percolates through the rich soil it picks up large quantities of mineral nutrients which are carried by the feeder streams into the lakes.

The high level of nutrient salts makes the Kamloops lakes exceptionally productive. Water weed and plant plankton abound and support huge quantities of aquatic invertebrates; the trout grow rapidly. Sometimes, however, the very richness of these lakes results in the death of a proportion of the trout stocks. In summer, when the air temperature may exceed 35°C, the bloom of aquatic plant life can result in bacterial decomposition that removes the bulk of oxygen from the water: a trout-kill then results.

In winter, when the lakes are iced over and oxygen from the air cannot diffuse into the water, the slow decomposition of dead plant material may similarly result in oxygen levels that are dangerously low. On occasions a lake may lose its entire trout population; but the stock is replaced naturally when young trout that have spent the first year or two of life in their natal feeder streams enter the lake.

The Kamloops trout breed in spring. Through the winter the lakes are locked in ice, and when the thaw comes the mature fish—usually four years of age or more—run the feeder streams or outflow. There in May they spawn and, in the majority of cases, die. The trout fry emerge in summer. Some move slowly through the stream to the lake, but others remain in the river, possibly for just one year, but in some cases for life. Those that enter the lake grow quickly before the ice of winter brings virtual hibernation.

The immature trout show very different growth rates in the lake and the river. By the age of two years a lake

RIGHT
A Kamloops Lake rainbow trout. Rainbows reach great sizes in the lakes of the Kamloops region, whose waters are rich in invertebrate foods.

Specimen study/watercolour

Working drawing/pencil

Kamloops Rainbow Trout
Salmo gairdneri gairdneri

Kamloops will be at least ten inches long; a river trout much smaller. A two-year-old from Lundbom Lake was found to have grown to $14\frac{1}{2}$ inches, while a fish from the same spawning, taken from a nearby stream, was but $3\frac{1}{2}$ inches in length. Why do not all the trout fry migrate to the lake, where the feeding is clearly so much better than the spawning stream? Whatever the reason, the result is a reserve population in the stream that can restock the lake naturally should catastrophic deoxygenation wipe out the lake stock.

The size and abundance of Kamloops trout have made the lakes a mecca for anglers. There are tales from the early years of cowboys catching 300 fish in a day on the most basic tackle made from a willow stick with a piece of string tied to the end, and a single fly. There were also some massive trout. In 1932 one was taken from Jewel Lake that may have been the biggest trout ever caught: though its weight was not officially verified, it was reported as scaling 56 lbs. As recently as September 1977 a fish of 25 lbs 2 oz was taken on dry fly from Kootenay Lake.

Decades of fishing pressure by 'sporting' anglers, commercial fisherman, and more recently huge numbers of visiting anglers, have taken their toll on the main Kamloops lakes. The effects of over-fishing have been exacerbated by mining waste polluting some waterways; spawning streams have also been damaged by erosion and silting due to deforestation of the river banks. The result is that for many years the Kamloops lakes have been unable to maintain their trout stocks by natural output.

Artificial hatcheries now produce trout for the major lakes, in many cases successfully. Other waters, especially lakes set high in the mountains, which the wild trout never

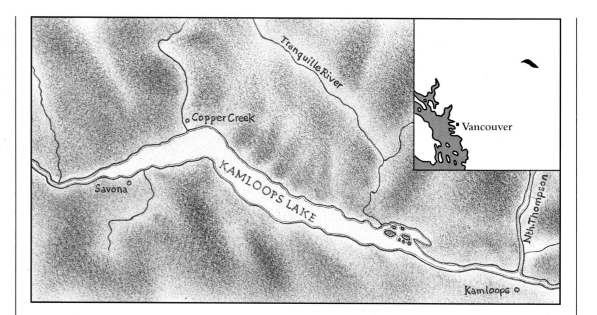

colonized, have been stocked with Kamloops trout. However, some have been overstocked, with disastrous effects on the lake invertebrate populations and the trout themselves.

The wilderness that was once a part of the Kamloops region is slowly disappearing as growing numbers of American, Canadian and European anglers despoil the lake shores. Along the shore of some of the more accessible lakes lie piles of rubbish—empty rusting food cans, beer bottles, plastic bags, discarded nylon fishing line, and general litter. From the lake comes a continuous drone of outboard motors and the wind drifts the stench of spilt engine oil and fuel. The Kamloops is, indeed, a wilderness in danger.

ABOVE
Kamloops Lake lies just below the fork of the North and South Thompson Rivers.

Fed by the snowmelt from the Caribou and Selkirk Mountains, Kamloops Lake is exceptionally productive. The Kamloops trout is the largest of all the lake rainbows.

THE CRESCENT LAKE TROUT

Set in the north of Olympic National Park in Washington State, Lake Crescent is a large lake covering more than 5,000 acres and exceeding 600 feet in depth. Two species of wild trout are native to the lake, a variety of rainbow trout which was named *Salmo gairdneri beardsleei* by D. S. Jordan in 1896 and a lake form of the coastal cutthroat trout *Salmo clarki clarki*, which has the varietal name *crescentis*.

Distinguishing between the two was not easy even when they were both abundant, up to the early years of the 20th century. The Crescent Lake rainbow trout, also known as the blueback and Beardslee trout, tended to be much larger, attaining weights in excess of 15 lbs, while the speckled trout (as the cutthroat of the lake were known) reached only half that size. But through most of the year their coloration was very similar, a dark steel-grey or blue with different amounts of spotting; the cutthroat had heavier spotting than the rainbow. Only at the onset of the breeding season did the differences between the two really become apparent, when the cutthroat developed its characteristic red flashes on the throat and the rainbow exhibited its iridescent flanks.

Identification today is considerably more difficult. Between 1920 and 1975 stocks of several other varieties of rainbow trout and cutthroat trout were introduced into Lake Crescent. During the 1970s it was possible to catch trout of almost all shapes, sizes and colours without being certain that any individual was either the native rainbow or cutthroat. Doubts were expressed that these native strains could ever have survived in a pure state.

However, research carried out in the early 1980s by Bryan Pierce of the Colorado State University demonstrated that both species of wild trout have survived in the lake, genetically intact. No further stocking of non-native fish is being carried out, and as anglers remove the remaining stock of introduced fish, Crescent Lake might yet revert to the days when it had just its two forms of wild trout.

These two very close species co-existed without interbreeding. Old reports demonstrate that the two had quite different ecologies in the lake. The cutthroats spawned before the rainbow trout and in a different place: the rainbows spawned in the mouth of the Lyre River, the outflowing stream, while most of the cutthroats bred in the inflowing Barnes Creek or else in the lower reaches of the Lyre River.

Some degree of competition was further avoided by the young cutthroats remaining in their natal streams for the first two years of life, while the rainbow trout fry entered the lake immediately after leaving the redds. However, both the Crescent Lake trout fed on the same food sources: small insects initially, and then on a diet of fish (notably, the kokanee, a form of landlocked sockeye salmon), which resulted in fast growth rates.

90

THE YELLOWSTONE LAKE TROUT

Set in the midst of the world's first National Park, Yellowstone Lake lies at 7,731 feet and covers an area of almost 140 square miles. The prolonged winters at this altitude keep the lake frozen over for virtually half of the year, from about November to May. The surrounding countryside, a mosaic of pine and fir forest, alpine meadows and rocky bluffs, is blanketed through winter with up to five feet of level snow and drifts that are far deeper. In spring the snow is quick to melt: high summer temperatures develop even at this altitude.

The streams that enter Yellowstone Lake carry little in the way of mineral salts. So the lake produces relatively small populations of aquatic invertebrates. Midge larvae and pupae are the most abundant; on a warm summer evening clouds of adult midges that have hatched from the water form mating columns resembling plumes of smoke drifting along the lake shore. In the shallow lake margins freshwater shrimps or scuds are amongst the most numerous large invertebrates, while in the surface layers of the deeper water, clouds of tiny zooplankton (crustaceans such as *Daphnia*) graze the summer bloom of algal phytoplankton.

Long winters and a relatively low level of food production mean that the wild cutthroat trout in Yellowstone Lake do not grow big. Most scale less than a pound; a two pounder is a large fish; a trout of more than three pounds is a giant. It is worth noting, however, that Yellowstone cutthroat trout have grown up to 16 lbs weight when introduced to other lakes, such as Red Eagle Lake in Montana, that formerly held no trout.

The native cutthroat wait until the May melt before they run from the lake to spawn in the feeder streams. The spawning run is very rapid, as the fish have ripe ovaries and testes when they set off on the journey upstream. Within a month of leaving the lake they have paired, cut their redds in the riverbed gravel, laid and fertilized their eggs, and returned downstream to the lake. It has been estimated that up to 20 per cent die during this mating period; but those that survive quickly regain their condition through the summer and early autumn, and most are ready to make a second spawning run by the following spring.

In the warm summer temperatures the eggs develop rapidly. After about five weeks the fry swim up through the gravel, and most head straight downstream to the lake. A small proportion remain in the spawning streams, however: a reserve population that could survive a catastrophe destroying the lake's stock. The young fish that remain in the river usually move down to the lake the following spring, though a few remain in the streams for up to two years.

In the lake the fry and smaller trout move to the deeper water where they feed almost entirely on plankton or food that has drifted out from the shallow margins. The larger and older fish concentrate in the shallower water around the shore, feeding on more substantial invertebrates such as the abundant midge larvae and pupae and shrimps, or on insects blown on to the water from the surrounding forest and scrub. In many lakes throughout the world the larger trout would prey very heavily on their smaller relatives; but the Yellowstone cutthroat is neither a cannibal nor a fish-eater.

The Yellowstone trout is the most thriving wild form of cutthroat. No other variety has ever been introduced into the lake, so the Yellowstone trout has neither suffered from

YELLOWSTONE CUTTHROAT TROUT
Salmo clarki bouvieri

competition nor had its genetic structure contaminated through hybridization. The lake also has been spared from commercial exploitation by net fishing. The survival of the Yellowstone cutthroat almost certainly owes much to the harsh conditions that prevail through the long winter, and to the protection provided by the National Park.

Yellowstone Park is famous for its hot springs and geysers. In the late 19th and early years of the 20th century, anglers liked to fish from the shore close to one of the hot springs. When a trout was hooked it was lifted from the water without a net and swung directly into the spring, where it died immediately. After a couple of minutes the rod was again lifted, this time with the trout ready for eating. This practice was made illegal in 1912. But elsewhere in the world wild trout stocks were being over-exploited and allowed to dwindle. It is a pity that other lakes that once held their own special strain of wild trout were not given similar protection.

ABOVE

Yellowstone Lake lies beneath the Absaroka Mountains of the Rockies, *entirely within the borders of Wyoming's Yellowstone National Park.*

CHAPTER FOUR

WILD SEA TROUT

Although the vast majority of trout spawn in the gravel of river beds, the sea-going gene may well be present in all trout varieties. It can indeed be argued that all trout are sea trout by ancestry because, over the past 10,000 years or so, most of our rivers and lakes were colonised by trout from the sea. Thus, the argument goes, those trout that live their entire lives today in freshwater are just sea trout that do not go to sea, as did their ancestors. Furthermore, the genes controlling the sea-going habit can still be activated in some lake and river trout. When brown trout from Loch Leven were put into inland waters of New Zealand and the Falkland Islands, they soon produced sea-going progeny that subsequently colonised other lakes and rivers.

The process continues today, as artificial stocking grows more common. In parts of northern Europe, river rainbow trout have already produced the sea-going steelhead: as recently as 1988 a 14 lb steelhead was caught in a stream in northern England. This fish had, presumably, developed from an introduced rainbow trout which had run to sea and then, after two years of sea-feeding, made a spawning run back into fresh-water. Similarly, in the northeastern USA and southeast Canada, introduced brown trout have spawned a strain of the Atlantic sea trout. Thus it is quite possible that, when an angler catches a large steelhead on the Columbia River or Fraser River, or a big Atlantic sea trout in Norway or Scotland, the parents of that fish were not sea-going, but freshwater trout.

Once the adaptation is made, however, it is almost impossible to detect the origins of an individual, for sea trout are remarkably consistent in shape and colour. The steelhead, sea-run cutthroat and Atlantic sea trout vary in size, depending upon the duration of sea-feeding and the richness of their feeding grounds; but they do not have the variety found in lake and river forms. Steelheads are similar from Alaska to the Gulf of Mexico; Atlantic sea trout vary in little but size from Western Ireland to Scandinavia. The distinctions once made between the 'eastern' sea trout of England, the 'Cambrian sea trout' of Wales and the 'western' sea trout of Ireland and western Scotland reflected differences of size and 'build': the consequences of diet rather than genetic variation.

For a special strain or subspecies of trout to evolve, the population must be isolated from all others over a long period, so that selective pressures can mould them into a distinct form adapted to their own particular water. At sea, no such isolation of a separate trout population can occur: the steelheads or sea-run cutthroats born in one river will mix freely with those from adjacent rivers. And although most sea trout eventually return to spawn in the river of their birth, some do not. Thus there is a small but continuous interchange of genes from one population of sea trout to the next.

However, all sea trout are clearly separated from the freshwater forms of their own species by their life history. Steelheads spawn in late winter and spring, but for cutthroats and Atlantic sea trout the breeding season is usually during early winter, in October, November and December, when the adult sea trout pair up in small gravel-bedded streams. After a brief courtship the female cuts into the gravel with scything slashes of her tail to form a redd deep enough to hold the eggs. With the cock fish lying close alongside her, she sheds a stream of round pink eggs into the redd; the male then moves forward and ejects a stream of milt, which contains the sperm that fertilizes the eggs. The female then flicks loose gravel over the eggs.

Sometimes a female may cut two or more redds, so that if one is predated, or the eggs are lost because a second female sea trout or salmon cuts into the same gravel, or the redd becomes

LEFT

Sea trout on their breeding redds. This pair may die following the rigours of spawning; but life continues in the gravel.

Night study/pastel

iced up, some eggs may still survive. After completing the act of reproduction the spent pair, now known as kelts, usually move off downstream into deeper water where they may rest for some time before heading back to the sea.

Some streams, or even parts of streams, are used by many pairs of sea trout, while other streams are ignored by all save, possibly, an occasional pair. On one major river system in northern England, just three becks hold the vast majority of the breeding sea trout, while scores of apparently similar streams have few. On one stream up to 1,400 pairs have spawned along a quarter of a mile reach. Likewise in the steelhead and sea-run cutthroat trout rivers of Oregon, Washington, British Columbia and Alaska huge numbers of sea trout spawn in particular river tributaries, and avoid others. Some sea trout share their spawning grounds with salmon, but in many rivers, the salmon choose different spawning areas from the trout.

Where there are spawning streams for trout and salmon close to large cities or towns poachers may take fish from the redds before they have spawned. Poachers can make a very quick profit from such streams and, in a short time, almost wipe out the fishery. So in many regions bailiffs must camp by the water to protect the fish when they are most vulnerable. Looking at the problem through human eyes, it would seem better for the fish to scatter throughout the river system. But presumably they have chosen these nursery areas over the years because there is an advantage in doing so: possibly the waters provide better conditions for the early stages of the sea trout life than other parts of the river.

It is difficult to estimate what proportion of sea trout kelts survive the long journey back to sea. But survival rates seem to be significantly higher than for the salmon, where mortality among cock kelts is 90 per cent or more, and among females at

least 70 per cent for the Atlantic salmon and 100 per cent in the Pacific sockeye. Huge shoals of sea trout kelts are sometimes found in February and March resting in deep slow pools in the river's lower reaches; where there is a large lake on the river system, the kelts will often lie there as they recover from the trauma of spawning. In spring they move off to sea where they feed, restore wasted tissues and form more eggs or sperm before making another spawning run into freshwater. But there is evidence that fish that have once spawned never regain the condition they had when they first ran the river. Sea trout caught as they are moving upstream on their second spawning run are generally 10–20 per cent lighter in weight than fish of the same length making the journey for the first time, and the quality of their flesh is often very poor.

For the first two or three years of their lives, sea trout are identical in appearance and behaviour to river trout. In summer they hunt shrimps, larvae and nymphs from the riverbed, and rise to take flies from the surface; in winter they hide amongst stones. But when the parr reach their maximum size, sea trout and freshwater trout diverge. In river varieties, the dark blue-grey parr marks disappear and the fish take on adult coloration, but in sea trout the parr lose their browns and reds and turn silver. They are now recognisable as smolts, ready at last to head out to the open sea.

Internally, the young sea trout have made a further physiological adaptation that will allow them to cope with salt water. In nature pure water will always pass from less concentrated solutions to more concentrated solutions. This has a crucial relevance to the sea trout, for while fresh water is less

LEFT
Northumberland's River Tyne, once ruined by industrial pollution, now sees large runs of Atlantic sea trout.

RIGHT
An Atlantic sea trout at night, in the shallow headwaters of its natal river.

concentrated than the trout's body fluids, sea water is much more concentrated. As a result, the sea trout must adapt to cope with a steady loss of body fluids as soon as it enters the sea.

While the parr is still in fresh water, it is constantly gaining fluids. River water enters the parr's body wherever there are thin membranes (such as the gills and inside of the mouth) by a process known to biologists as osmosis. If this water were not excreted, the cells of its body would literally burst. The fish living in freshwater uses its kidney system to remove all this water, excreting large amounts of dilute urine almost continuously. In salt water, osmosis occurs in the other

direction, and the body of the fish loses water to the sea. Were this to continue, the fish would die from dehydration. So instead of excreting continuously, the sea trout drinks large quantities of sea water and excretes very concentrated urine; special glands in its gills also excrete salt. So it replaces the body fluids it loses by osmosis with desalinated sea water.

Sometime in spring, having acquired their silver livery and made their physiological adaptation, the smolts move downstream, pass through the estuary and on into the sea. There their lifestyle remains something of a mystery, for fishery scientists have devoted far less time to the migrations of sea trout

THE ATLANTIC SEA TROUT

For the angler and naturalist, the Atlantic sea trout is quite different from the river or lake brown trout. When it returns from the sea it is a bright bar of silver, dripping with tide lice. Bigger specimens can never be confused with the freshwater trout: in fact, to the uninitiated, they more resemble the Atlantic salmon. Many an angler has shown off a 5 lb salmon, only to learn that the square tail, long jaws, and structure of the anal fin show it to be a sea trout.

Naturalists of the 19th century described several 'species' of Atlantic sea trout. As well as *Salmo trutta*, the sea trout of Scotland and Ireland, they identified *Salmo cambricus*, the sewen or sewin of Wales, southern England and Scandinavia; *Salmo gallivensis*, the Galway sea trout; *Salmo brachypoma*, the eastern sea trout of the British rivers Tweed, Forth and Ouse; and *Salmo argenteus*, the silvery salmon of the Atlantic rivers of France.

These 'species' had little in the way of scientific merit, being identified and described from very few specimens and on fairly tenuous grounds. The Reverend Houghton himself failed to obtain a specimen of the eastern sea trout despite much trying, and was forced to borrow Günter's pickled specimen from the Natural History Museum. Eventually all Atlantic sea trout were given the name *Salmo fario*; but modern fish biologists have considered that brown trout and Atlantic sea trout are one and the same species; so today they are officially clumped together as *Salmo trutta*.

Yet if, as seems likely, Atlantic sea trout are merely a migratory form of brown trout, the question remains: why do some become sea trout and not others? Obviously this is not a matter of a small trout deciding to visit the coast.

Those trout parr that will become sea trout go through an extra stage of development that lake or river trout omit from their life cycle: the smolt stage. They develop salt-excreting glands and the characteristic silver coat of the smolt. This extra stage must be genetically induced. Genes from sperm and egg decide that, at two or three years of age, the individual will develop into a smolt and become a sea trout.

Furthermore, sea trout produce more sea trout. The evidence comes from hatchery stations, where returning sea trout are stripped of their ova and milt, and their progeny are raised in controlled conditions and later released to boost the output of natural spawning. These sea trout off-spring develop the smolt stage and head off to sea. Hatchery-raised brown trout do not: they grow from parr into river or lake trout without the smolt stage.

So it would seem that within some varieties of freshwater brown trout, including the trout of the River Thames and Loch Leven, remain the latent genes of sea-going trout. Such genes could be inherited from the original stock of trout that colonised these waters from the sea, thousands of years ago. If so, these genes may require a trigger before they confer the sea-going trait.

Hunger could be enough. The greatest Atlantic sea trout rivers produce little food, and their resident brown trout tend to be tiny: rivers like the Welsh Dovey and Conwy, the Cumbrian Esk, the Border Esk, Scotland's Spey and Loch Maree, some of the barren Irish and Hebridean lochs, and the glacier-fed rivers of western and northern Norway. Possibly it is scarcity of food, a near-starvation diet, that triggers the genes which turn the brown trout into a sea-going fish.

RIGHT
An Atlantic sea trout. The bronze sheen reveals that this hen fish has spent a week or two in freshwater; while at sea, the scales would be bright silver.

Specimen study/watercolour

ATLANTIC SEA TROUT

Salmo trutta trutta

than of the economically more valuable salmon. What evidence there is suggests that the sea trout smolts do not move as far out into the Atlantic or Pacific oceans as the salmon. Instead they fan out along the coast, forming huge shoals in certain favoured areas. Large numbers of Atlantic sea trout have been encountered feeding on sprats, sand eels and young herrings in the North Sea, off the English coast around East Anglia and off the Low Countries coast between Holland and Jutland: others in the English Channel between the Isle of Wight and Land's End.

It seems likely that the North Sea trout are from the rivers of eastern Scotland (the Spey, Ythan and others) or southern Scandinavia (including the Swedish Em). The Channel trout probably originate from the small sea trout rivers of southern England. However, some trout move much further from their natal rivers. Hugh Falkus, in his book *Sea Trout Fishing*, reported a kelt tagged in Devon's River Axe, in south-west England, that was recaptured 166 days later in the estuary of the River Tweed on the Scottish border. That fish had travelled a minimum of 580 miles through the Channel and the North Sea. Another noted by Falkus travelled at least 244 miles in 174 days.

Other high concentrations of Atlantic sea trout are well known around the shores of the Orkneys and Shetlands, the Outer Hebrides and the west coast of Ireland. Here the fish move close inshore on the tide, pursuing small fish, crabs and shrimps. These trout almost certainly originate from the rivers of northern and western Scotland, Ireland and perhaps northern England.

Most studies on the life of sea trout confirm the generally short distance of their journeys. One Swedish survey showed that few Atlantic sea trout travelled more than thirteen miles from the estuary. Similarly, the sea-run cutthroat trout rarely moves more than a few miles from the natal river estuary; the

current record, for a tagged fish, is about 80 miles. Steelheads may travel much further. Although one study reported a maximum journey of nineteen miles from the river estuary, shoals have been known to travel a few hundred miles. Individuals have even been encountered in the Pacific more than 2000 miles from land.

At sea the trout feed on a wide variety of marine life. The smolts initially concentrate on crustaceans in the plankton: small shrimps, and the larval stages of crabs, lobsters and prawns. As they grow, they turn increasingly to a fish diet, dominated by inshore species such as sprats, sand eels, herrings, smelts, sculpins and sparlings. Where the feeding grounds include extensive tidal sandflats, large crustaceans including crabs and shrimps feature in the diet.

The marine trout is a hunter. Off the coast of Oregon and California, flocks of terns and gulls can be observed diving for small fish that have been forced to the sea surface by steelheads and cutthroats. As the tide flows into sandy bays and rocky inlets, shoals of swirling sea trout are often close behind in pursuit of their lesser prey. Sea life is a time of gluttony: it is by no means unusual to land an Atlantic sea trout from a Hebridean storm beach or an Irish sea lough that is stuffed with small fish literally oozing from its throat.

The rich feeding results in very rapid growth of the smolts, which are now properly known as post-smolts. A proportion of these post-smolts (100 per cent in sea-run cutthroats and up to 60 per cent of Atlantic sea trout) return to the river after only a few months at sea. These are known as herling, peal, finnock, whitling or juniors. Many remain in the river through the winter, and some may spawn. Atlantic sea trout herling may spend only a few weeks of autumn in the river before heading seawards again.

RIGHT
Sea trout waters of the northeast Atlantic, looking from the Scottish mainland across the North Minch channel to the Isle of Skye.

An Atlantic sea trout; the hooked lower jaw, or 'kype' reveals this to be a male fish. The square tail fin, the broad 'wrist' at the base of the tail, and the long jaw that extends to behind the eye are the features that most obviously distinguish Atlantic sea trout from salmon.

Measured drawing/pencil and wash

Those post-smolts that remain at sea, and the herling that run back to sea quickly after a brief return to the river, continue to grow quickly. By the end of their first year in the sea they may be almost twice the size they were on leaving fresh water; now they are properly termed sea trout. A year later they might reach the 2 lb mark, and the longer the fish remain at sea the bigger they get. An 11 lb Atlantic sea trout caught in the River Spey in 1983 had spent about seven years feeding at sea; in 1989 the British rod record, for a fish taken from the River Tweed in 1983, stood at 20 lbs exactly. Much bigger fish are caught in Scandinavia: on the Swedish Em the record is 32 lbs 5½ oz and in a single day one angler took six fish at a total of 113 lbs.

The steelheads of the Pacific coast of North America rival Scandinavian sea trout. A small proportion of steelheads return to the river after only a few months at sea, like the herling of the Atlantic sea trout, but even after this short spell of sea-feeding they weigh 2 lbs or more. The majority return after one or two years of sea-feeding, when they weigh between 5 and 12 lbs. These are probably fish that have not migrated very long distances, but have drifted along the coast in search of food. The long-distance migrants return after at least three years at sea, reaching weights of 20 lbs and more. There are reports of steelhead scaling the 50 lb mark; but the best authenticated record is of a 42 lbs 2 oz fish caught on Alaska's Bell Island by David White on 22 June 1970. A 33 lb steelhead caught on the Kispiox in British Columbia by Karl Mausser in 1967 is still the record caught on fly.

At some stage the urge to reproduce will drive all sea trout back to fresh water. Herling return after only a few months of sea feeding; other trout (possibly the bulk) make their first spawning run after two or three years at sea. The biggest fish will have spent many years at sea before heading back to freshwater. A study by the Irish fishery scientist Edward Fahy (*Child of the Tides*, 1985) suggested that herling do not necessarily return to their natal river, but to a river in the region of their birth. However, adult sea trout with two or more years at sea almost always return to the river of their birth. Fahy also confirmed the widely held view that trout find their way back by taste. It seems that each river has its own special flavour,

BELOW
Sea trout foods – sand-eels and other small fish – and the artificial lures used by anglers.

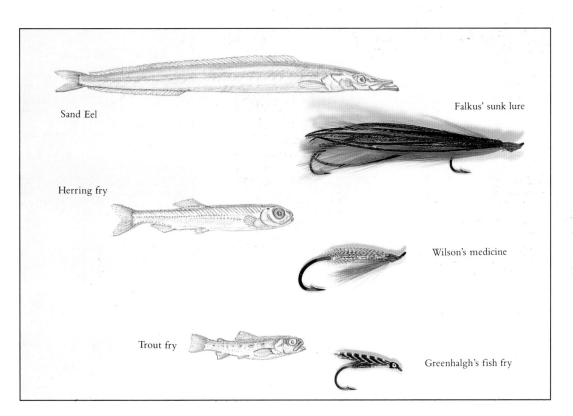

Sand Eel

Falkus' sunk lure

Herring fry

Wilson's medicine

Trout fry

Greenhalgh's fish fry

THE STEELHEAD TROUT

Until quite recently scientists classified the steelhead trout *Salmo gairdneri* separately from the freshwater rainbow trout of the Pacific coastal region of North America, which they named *Salmo irideus*. However, the steelhead is now regarded simply as a rainbow trout that spends part of its life cycle at sea. Thus, the steelhead and the freshwater rainbow trout are clumped together as the species *Salmo gairdneri*. However, those who have angled for both freshwater rainbows and steelheads will attest that the two varieties are quite different in appearance and behaviour.

The adult steelheads spawn in late winter and spring, when high water in the river systems, following the first snowmelts, enables the fish to reach the headwaters quickly and easily. During the winter these streams are often iced-up; in summer, the flow may be too small for the fish to complete their upstream migration. The fertilized eggs, hidden deep in gravel redds, are assured a good supply of oxygen-rich cold water as the snow melt continues during spring and early summer. And by the time the steelhead fry begin to seek food in the summer and early autumn, the river is at its most productive as far as insects are concerned.

Young steelhead trout grow rapidly. By the end of the year they may have reached five inches in length, and by their second birthday seven inches or more. At this stage, the steelhead parr are indistinguishable from the parr of freshwater rainbow trout that will never go to sea. But the following year, when they are seven to ten inches long, the steelhead parr become smolts. They lose their lavender-pink hue and attain a more silvery attire; quickly they move downstream to saltwater.

While sea-run cutthroat trout tend to remain in tidal waters close to the estuaries of their natal rivers, steelhead shoals will frequently travel a few hundred miles from their home river in search of marine foods. Some steelheads tagged as smolts in rivers in British Columbia have been reported from the seas around Kodiak Island in Alaska, and others have been reported by commercial fishing boats in mid-Pacific up to 2,5000 miles away from their natal rivers.

Some rivers have a reputation for producing big steelheads, others produce smaller fish. Even though they are all steelheads, the pattern does suggest that each river system has its own variety of steelhead. In his large work *Trout* (1979), Ernest Schweibert noted that the steelhead smolts from 'big fish rivers' made the longest migrations and spent an extra year feeding out at sea. Hence the greater size of these fish. However he also argued that the ecology of rivers such as the Columbia and Skeena influenced trout size, because the heavy flow of these rough rivers and the very large stones of the river bed meant that smaller steelheads could not breed there successfully. Only the older and much larger steelheads could mate, cut redds and spawn in these torrent-like conditions.

Because of their size and the spectacular rivers they inhabit, steelheads are possibly the most exciting trout to catch. However, this has to some extent been their undoing. During the 20th century the rivers of Oregon, Washington State, British Columbia and Alaska have attracted anglers from across the USA and Canada, and from Europe and the Far East. Steelheads have been a popular quarry: huge numbers have been taken with little recognition that the populations might one day suffer from over-fishing.

The outcome is that the steelhead stocks of many rivers

STEELHEAD TROUT
Salmo gairdneri trideus

THE WILD TROUT

Erratum

page 107

The correct spelling of the Linnaean classification for
Steelhead Trout is *Salmo gairdneri irideus*.

are now supplemented with fish raised in hatcheries. Bill Luch, author of *Steelhead Drift Fishing* (1976) put it this way: 'There are very few "wild" runs of steelhead trout left in the United States. Due mostly to the insane depredations of man, it has become necessary to artificially propagate these fish in order to preserve the runs. In other words, most steelheads today are not wild fish, but the product of the hatchery.'

A far better solution to the problem of over-fishing is to reduce fishing pressure. Measures to achieve this are now in force on many river systems: some areas are catch-and-release; elsewhere the angler is restricted to the number of fish that may be taken; and on some rivers (for example, the Dean River system of British Columbia) the number of fishing permits available to visiting anglers is severely restricted. Surely this is the answer to conserving wild trout populations: to keep the angling pressure at a level the trout stocks can sustain.

ABOVE

The Columbia River flows several hundred miles down from the Rockies to enter the Pacific on the Washington-Oregon Border. As the snows melt at the end of winter, large steelheads swim up-river to spawn in the headwaters.

The River Spey, one of Scotland's premier Atlantic sea trout and salmon rivers, flows northeast from the Grampian Highlands into the Moray Firth.

which the fish homes in on when it gets close to the river estuary.

On their first run into the river, the trout may move only a short distance upstream, completing the rest of their journey to the headwater spawning becks in a series of short stages. Unlike salmon, which require a good flow of water before they can ascend, sea trout can move upstream on very low water, splashing their way from pool to pool through shallow runs

which barely cover them. However, the large runs of fish usually wait for a falling spate before running into the river.

When they reach fresh water, sea trout are still quite silver. The larger Atlantic sea trout are often confused with Atlantic salmon, which they resemble closely (indeed the common name of the Atlantic sea trout is 'salmon trout'). The presence of sea lice, usually low on the body close to the anal fin, indicates that a fish has been only two or three days in freshwater. But the longer sea trout remain in the river, the duller grows their silver sheen. Flecks of pink, copper and brown appear and proliferate until the sea trout attains its darker spawning livery.

There has been much debate whether migratory trout feed in the river after they have run from the tide. Herling certainly do: on most rivers they can be watched taking sedges or spent spinners from the water surface, and caught on a dry fly imitation of these. Larger sea-run trout may also feed; on the big loughs of western Ireland a dapped daddy-long-legs is frequently taken by sea trout when lake brownies were the intended quarry. Even big sea trout will occasionally take food, unlike the salmon which rarely feeds in freshwater.

However, the food intake is certainly minimal. As Hugh Falkus pointed out, no river is productive enough to sustain a run of big sea trout. If they fed in earnest they would rapidly wipe out the stocks of parr and small trout, and would snap up every fly that floated over them. That sea trout (with the exception of herling) do not feed seriously when they return to the river is borne out by stomach analyses. In a study of 522 sea trout caught in British rivers, only 14 contained identifiable food remains; and of 46 taken in Norwegian rivers, not one had food in its stomach.

For the steelhead, however, some feeding may be essential to survival. These large trout often share the same river systems with the Pacific salmon, which all die immediately after the act of spawning is complete. The river bed and banks are strewn with rotting salmon corpses on which gulls, bears and other scavengers gorge themselves. Less than half of all steelhead kelts (up to about 40 per cent, depending on the river system and year) survive the rigours of spawning: slowly they drift downstream and reach the sea where the rich feeding enables them to recover.

Such a relatively high survival rate is probably due to the adult steelheads taking some food in the river. In the estuary they will eat crabs, prawns and small fish, and as they move upstream they will feed on river invertebrates and fish fry. After spawning they will take the eggs of other salmonids that have been washed from the redds, as well as invertebrates and small fish. Judging from stomach analyses the amount of such food that they take is not huge; but it probably makes the difference between death and survival. The salmon take no food at all after leaving the sea and entering the estuary; and they all die.

Those steelheads that successfully reach the sea after completing their winter spawning run usually return to the river to breed again in summer. They reach the estuary between late spring and early October. The relatively short period of sea-feeding allows them to rebuild tissues that have been wasted, and to produce eggs and sperm for a second spawning. Rarely is there enough time for the fish to grow larger than they were on their initial return to freshwater.

Few fish spend part of their lives in freshwater and part in the sea, passing at least twice through estuaries. Sea trout and salmon are therefore uniquely vulnerable to anything that damages the marine ecosystem, the freshwater ecosystem or the estuary that links the two. They require cool, well-oxygenated, clean water during spawning and in the pre-smolt stages. They need a clean estuary, to allow migration to and from the sea. They demand a marine environment which is prolific in small fish and crustaceans, so that they can grow sufficient reserves of muscle and fat to carry them back to the river to spawn.

Consequently, sea trout and salmon are probably more

RIGHT
Small shoals of sea trout hunting in rich coastal waters.

Pastel and wash

sensitive than any other fish to fluctuations in water quality. Their presence is a good indication of the healthy state of rivers, estuaries and the sea; but their numbers rapidly decline where waters are polluted. Today the feeding grounds of most sea trout populations are under some threat. Worst affected are the North Sea, Baltic Sea and Irish Sea, home waters of the Atlantic sea trout, which suffer from the dumping of organic waste, toxic metals, chemicals and other industrial effluents. There are international agreements to reduce these hazards to sea trout and all other marine life, but currently the damage is increasing.

Of greater concern, in the long term, is the potential impact of commercial overfishing of the smaller fish species that form the sea trout's main diet. Fishing fleets have virtually exhausted the stocks of larger seafish in inshore waters, and many boats are now fishing for lesser fish. Already there are reports that the Atlantic sand eel stocks are suffering from overfishing. Birds that prey on these small fish have been dramatically affected: ornithologists have noted a massive decline of breeding success in kittiwakes, puffins, guillemots, terns and other sea birds. Low stocks of sand eels result in the sea birds being unable to find enough food for themselves and their chicks. Sea trout stocks could be suffering for the same reason: detection is difficult because the fish are less visible than the sea birds.

Estuary pollution has completely exterminated sea trout in the worst affected river systems, but the process is not necessarily irreversible. Two of the world's filthiest rivers, the Mersey and Rhine, no longer have runs of sea trout—the fish cannot get through the estuaries. But their headwaters could still support the immature and returning sea trout. Where rivers and estuaries have been cleaned up in recent years, the sea trout have quickly returned.

However, even when the sea, estuary and headwaters are clean and productive, humans still endanger the survival of sea trout in some rivers. The rod-and-line angler is unlikely to inflict long term damage on a stock of sea trout, but the poacher most certainly can. For the domestic consumer there seems no difference between a pink-fleshed, brightly-coloured sea trout and a salmon; and large sea-run trout are often sold as salmon.

Consequently, sea trout, like salmon, are hounded by criminals: illegally netted at sea, in estuaries and in river pools; even blown up with explosives. Worse still, some poachers use poisons such as cyanide to kill the fish. This wipes out all river life, and a trout pool will take years to recover. In the most heavily populated parts of their range, there is no doubt that sea trout would be extinct (or almost so) without a massive supplementation of the wild stock with hatchery-bred fish.

THE COASTAL CUTTHROAT TROUT

Of the three varieties of sea trout, only the sea-run cutthroat *Salmo clarki clarki* is smaller than its freshwater relatives. The steelhead grows much larger than the average lake and river rainbow; the Atlantic sea trout far outstrips the average brown trout. It is easy to assume that because the sea is so bountiful in food resources, any sea-going trout will quickly grow big and fat. Yet the average sea-run cutthroat weighs little more than a pound, three pounders are quite scarce, and a five pounder is, in angling terms, the fish of a lifetime. River cutthroats are of comparable size, and lake cutthroats may grow much bigger.

Sea-run cutthroat trout are widespread along the Pacific coast of North America, from Alaska to the Queen Charlotte Islands and British Columbia (including Vancouver Island) south through the United States seaboard to California. Few rivers and streams are without them. Smolt migration occurs in late April and May in California, in May and June in Oregon and Washington State, and up to the end of July in British Columbia and Alaska. These smolts join into shoals with those cutthroats that have previously spawned to feed on smaller fish such as Pacific herrings and anchovies, and crustaceans such as shrimps and euphausid prawns. Within three months of reaching the sea, an eight inch cutthroat smolt will have attained a length of twelve inches.

Unlike Atlantic sea trout and steelheads, however, cutthroat trout never move far from their natal river estuary; and rarely will they cross areas of very deep seawater, preferring to hug the shoreline and feed over sand and gravel in little more than ten feet of water.

Furthermore, they spend far less time in the sea than either of the other varieties. With the exception of a small proportion of cutthroats from the north of their range (Alaska and, possibly, British Columbia), the entire sea-run population returns to freshwater in late summer and autumn.

The older and larger fish, which have spawned in previous years, return to the estuaries first. By September all have left the sea and are in the estuaries or have run the river. They continue to feed throughout this return journey, taking crustaceans and small fish such as sculpins from the estuary, and caddis larvae and stonefly and mayfly nymphs from the freshwater. Once they have reached the spawning streams, feeding virtually ceases as mating begins.

Though not all cutthroats spawn on their first return to freshwater, they will remain in the river throughout the spawning period, until the whole population moves down to the sea once more in April and May. Thus the sea-run cutthroat has on average only four or five months of sea-feeding each year after leaving the river as a smolt.

In the far north, however, some Alaskan sea-run cutthroat trout do overwinter in the sea following their initial seaward migration as smolts. Eight such fish, which made their maiden runs after a winter at sea weighed between $1\frac{3}{4}$ and $3\frac{1}{4}$ lbs. The smallest had spent two years in the river and was thus three years old when it was caught; the largest fish had spent three years in the river before it left for the sea and was thus four years old. A three year old cutthroat from the rivers of Oregon and Washington would weigh about $1\frac{1}{2}$ lb; and a $3\frac{1}{4}$ lb fish from these waters would be at least six years old.

Cutthroat trout in lakes and rivers can easily be

COASTAL CUTTHROAT TROUT
Salmo clarki clarki

identified by the red flashes on either side of the throat. In the sea-run form these markings are not so clear, just a slight flush of very pale orange or cream when the fish are in the sea and immediately after they have returned to freshwater. Superficially they resemble the freshwater rainbow or small herling steelhead. However, the more extensive spotting over the body of the cutthroat, with the exception of a narrow silver-white band on the underside between the pectoral and pelvic fins, is quite characteristic. For certain identification it is necessary to examine the tongue: the base of the tongue of the cutthroat has conspicuous hyoid teeth.

The colours change rapidly when the cutthroat returns to the river. Its silver flanks turn to yellow-brown; its pale blue-green back turns a darker olive green; the spotting becomes more conspicuous. Above all, the faint orange on the throat becomes a vivid rich orange-red, the mark of the cutthroat.

For many years, the sea-run cutthroat stocks were reduced in some waters by pollution, habitat destruction or over-fishing. Because the cutthroat was economically unimportant, no effort was made to supplement the natural spawning with hatchery reared fish. In *Sea-Run* (1979), Les Johnson of Gig Harbor, Washington State, described a happier prospect. At Alsea River in Oregon and on the coast near Manchester, Washington, are two hatcheries that raise cutthroats to smolt stage. Furthermore, throughout the range of the migratory cutthroat there is an increasing trend to impose bag limits and encourage catch-and-release. It is hoped that this trend will continue, for the little sea-run cutthroat deserves careful conservation.

ABOVE
The Columbia River estuary, through which thousands of steelhead and cutthroat smolts pass each year on their journey from freshwater to the sea.

CHAPTER FIVE
CONSERVING THE WILD TROUT

The saddest trait of modern man is that he selfishly takes from the world around him without much thought either for his fellow creatures or for the generations that will follow him. The fact that, during the present century, the rate of extinction of plants and animals has been higher than in any preceding century, and that the vast majority of these losses can be attributed directly to human activity *and were avoidable*, will testify through the rest of time that 20th century man was an environmental vandal. What hope then is there for conserving the wild trout?

Living in an aquatic environment that is highly vulnerable to any interference, the wild trout populations of the industrialised world have been repeatedly damaged by human pressures. The water that flows through lakes and rivers may have been affected by acid rain, by agricultural fertilizers or industrial effluents. The riverbed and banks may have been disturbed by damming, dredging or deforestation. And where the water passing downstream is contaminated, it may affect the estuary and even the sea, sometimes for miles around. Outflow from the Rhine, Europe's filthiest river, has destroyed much of the marine life over large areas of the southern North Sea.

Today both national and international efforts are being made to clean up those waters that have suffered from gross pollution since the Industrial Revolution. Man is becoming more 'environmentally conscious'. The general public are demanding that their countryside should be protected; that where lakes, rivers and seas are contaminated, efforts should be made to clean them up. Industries that cause pollution have had to respond. Often their action is slow. Sometimes the situation appears to worsen before it gets better. However, now that there are votes in 'green' issues, we are certain to see a reduction of direct water pollution over the next few decades.

Provided that some remnant population of wild trout survives when a lake or river is made clean, the fish can soon respond and begin to restock the water. Within a few years they can spread back to areas where formerly they could not live. The bull trout and sea trout of the River Tyne in Northern England were virtually exterminated by estuarine pollution during the first half of the present century, but the pollution was removed in the 1970s and both sea trout and bull trout currently are on the increase.

Acid rain is a more intractable problem, since the industrial gases that cause this form of pollution may have been carried many hundreds of miles before they reach the ground, dissolved in rain water. Gaseous emissions from Germany and the United Kingdom are destroying the life in lakes and rivers in Scandinavia; acid gases from lowland England are affecting the lakes and rivers of English and Scottish uplands; atmospheric pollutants from the industrial centres of the USA are damaging waters in the Canadian wildernesses. Industrialists, and the governments of industrialised countries, have been reluctant to act quickly to reduce the damage. After all, this would be extremely expensive and might benefit their neighbour's countryside but not their own. So although there are international agreements on controlling such pollution, they are very weak affairs giving the polluters many years to reduce the problem. It seems that acidification is likely to be a hazard well into the 21st century. In the meantime, more and more lakes and rivers will lose trout stocks and other aquatic life.

Yet pollution is no longer the biggest threat to wild trout. Paradoxically, there are probably more trout worldwide today than there have ever been before. Trout have been introduced to regions that formerly had no trout, such as New Zealand, Tasmania, South America and southern Africa. The in-

LEFT
Many trout waters are used both for storing and transporting timber, causing considerable damage to the river banks. Here as elsewhere, tree felling on steep hillsides has also led to soil erosion and wide-spread silting of the riverbed. Many wild trout populations have declined as a result.

RIGHT
Pollution of rivers and lakes with agricultural and industrial waste is destroying wild trout habitats all over the world.

troductions have produced feral stocks and, in many cases, because of the genetic variation within these stocks, the feral populations have diversified further, to produce varieties of lake trout, river trout and sea trout. Even in Europe, the natural range of the wild brown trout and its varieties, and in western North America, the natural ranges of the wild rainbow and cutthroat trout and their allies, there are possibly more trout today than there were a century or more ago. However, it is in these regions, the homelands of the truly wild trout, that the fish are most endangered. Although the total trout population may have increased, this is due less to environmental improvement than to the wholesale stocking of wild trout rivers and lakes with alien varieties. The numbers of wild trout have seriously declined, and are still falling.

Sea-going trout—the coastal cutthroat, steelhead and Atlantic sea trout—have probably been the least affected. Although there has been some reduction in population in parts of their ranges, and although the estuaries of some river systems are too polluted to allow the fish to pass between freshwater and the sea, sea trout overall are thriving. This situation is due, at least in part, to the economic value of sea trout waters, which are consequently accorded special protection. Populations are bolstered by fish of the pure sea trout variety raised in commercial hatcheries.

It is the freshwater varieties of trout that face the greatest danger. In the USA and Canada, the populations of many of the scientifically accepted varieties of wild trout have crashed since man arrived in the western wildernesses; many rivers have been taken over by introduced forms of trout or by hybrid populations. Ten of the fourteen forms of freshwater cutthroat trout are now so rare that they appear on either State or National lists of endangered animals. A century ago most were abundant. Likewise some varieties of rainbow trout. In his book *Native Trout of North America*, Robert H. Smith sadly describes the Apache trout and Gila trout as: 'Now very rare as pure populations'; and other forms such as the golden trout of Volcano Creek, the Gilbert golden trout and the mountain strain of the Kamloops trout as occurring only 'above barriers' which introduced, non-indigenous trout cannot pass.

The danger is exacerbated because those forms of North American freshwater trout that are thriving, such as the Yellowstone and the Snake River cutthroat, and the South Fork Kern River golden trout, have been used to stock waters vacated by the declining trout varieties. This has reduced the chances of the native trout ever recolonising their traditional ranges; and where the remnant has hybridized with the introduced trout, the genetic purity of these rare forms has been ruined.

The freshwater trout of Britain and Europe—the brown trout and their allies—have generally not suffered to the same extent as some of the North American varieties, though they have been excluded from part of their pre-Industrial Revolution range. Most clean lakes and rivers still have populations that are clearly identifiable as 'brown trout', and some lakes maintain their own quite special varieties. What we do not know is whether there were far more local varieties like the sonaghen and Loch Leven trout two hundred or more years ago. Nor do we know if forms such as the gillaroo, that are today known from just a handful of lakes, were once more widespread.

There is growing concern, however, in both North America and Europe, as rivers and lakes continue to be stocked with trout from hatcheries. On stocking day a wagon carrying several thousand trout may set out from the fish farm and disgorge its load into three, four or more completely separate river systems. This may satisfy the requirements of the anglers:

they now have plenty of trout to catch in their beat. And the fishery owner may be quite content because heavy artificial stocking means that plenty of permits will be sold. But these trout are not the native trout of that river; they are not wild trout.

In the worst cases, European brown trout are used to stock lakes in North America and American rainbow trout to stock rivers and lakes in Europe. But even where the local species is used, it is common practice to stock one lake or river with trout that have originated from other lakes and rivers. Current evidence suggests that this is wrong. If a wild trout lake or river cannot be stocked with its own strain of trout, it would be better not to stock at all, but to protect the natural head that remains until the population recovers.

Many controllers of wild trout fisheries have expressed an interest in deliberately restocking their waters using trout from other areas, with the aim of introducing 'new blood' into their wild stock. This strategy is entirely mistaken. The lake or river has taken several thousand years to produce its own wild trout, a variety uniquely adapted to its water. Altering the genetic constitution of this variety will almost certainly produce a head of fish that is less well adapted to that water.

Superficially, this might not seem to matter. There are trout in the water. The angler can catch them. The naturalist can see them rising to fly, and be confident that the water is clean enough to support a trout population. However, evidence is slowly accumulating that, in the long run, it does matter. Because the trend is to stock with large trout (often much larger than the wild trout of the same lake or river), the introduced fish

RIGHT
Bull trout feeding in the sandy waters of an estuary.

Pastel and wash

THE BULL TROUT

A variety of brown trout that was almost wiped out by pollution, the bull or 'slob' trout was classified as *Salmo eriox*, a species in its own right, by the early 19th century taxonomist William Yarrell in *A History of British Fish* (1841). Yarrell identified it on the basis of quite small anatomical features in the gill cover and tail structure. When other naturalists obtained specimens, the arguments began. Some remarked that the bull trout they had examined were ordinary sea trout; others that they were river brown trout. In retrospect it seems that the published descriptions of the bull trout—though precise enough in terms of body structure—missed one vital point: the most distinctive feature of the fish was its behaviour.

In the 19th and early 20th century, the bull trout was frequently seen in three rivers of northeast England and southeast Scotland: the Tweed, Tyne and Coquet. Writing in 1885, Scottish game angler Lord Home wrote: 'The bull trout has increased in numbers in the Tweed prodigiously within the last forty years, and to that increase I attribute the decrease of salmon trout. . . . The bull trout take the river at two seasons. The first shoal come up about the end of April and May. They are then small, weighing from two to four or five pounds. The second, and by far the most numerous shoal, come late in November. They then come up in thousands, and are not only in fine condition, but of much larger size, weighing from six to twenty pounds.'

Close observation finally revealed that the bull trout is a river brown trout that migrates downstream after spawning to live in the tidal estuary. Unlike sea trout, the bull trout does not go through a smolt stage, because it can cope with the brackish waters of the estuary without making the physiological adaptations needed for survival in sea water. Bull trout normally take on a sandy coloration which blends with the colour of the estuary water and substrate, just as river and lake brown trout become camouflaged to the waters that they inhabit.

Where the river is very clean from source to estuary, bull trout parrs will move down to the estuary to feed in the brackish water just as other brown trout move to the lower freshwater reaches. Clean river estuaries are often more productive than the higher freshwater reaches, with shoals of sea fish fry, shrimps, shore crabs, molluscs and marine worms. So trout that do move down to the estuary grow much larger and attain a more portly bull-like shape than those that remain in freshwater.

Where an estuary becomes polluted, no trout can stay there through the spring and summer months, even though sea-going trout might be able to run quickly to and from the open sea. So few rivers in Europe have estuarine bull trout today. Some, like the Tyne, lost virtually all their bull trout when the estuaries became polluted early in the 20th century. But where pollution has been cleaned away, bull trout are gradually returning to some estuaries. Today they are occasionally seen not only in the Tweed, Tyne and Coquet, but in the clean sandy rivers of north and west Scotland, Wales, northwest England, Ireland and Norway.

RIGHT
A bull trout, showing the pale sandy coloration and bold spotting that help camouflage the fish in the murky water of an estuary. The heavy build results from a diet of fish fry and crustaceans.

Specimen study/watercolour

LEFT

An English lake being stocked with triploid trout, produced artificially by chromosomal manipulation. Such fish should only be put into water – like this – with no wild trout population, for they quickly grow large enough to take the best lies, devour smaller wild fish, and even follow the wild trout on to their redds and eat their eggs.

THE HUMAN IMPACT ON WILD TROUT STOCKS

CAUSE	EFFECT
POLLUTION	
Untreated or poorly treated organic effluent sewage, slurry, waste from paper mills and wood-pulp factories, waste milk from dairies	Deoxygenation of water, resulting in the death of trout and other aquatic animals
Toxic chemical effluent organo-chlorine residues from chemical industry, lead from mine waste	Poisoning of trout and all other aquatic animal life
Fertilizers especially nitrates and phosphates from farmland	Eutrophication leading to deoxygenation of water. This may result in the death or movement of trout; but in small amounts such pollution can increase the productivity of the water
ACIDIFICATION	
'acid rain' and 'acid runoff' from industrial gaseous emissions and high density conifer planting which also increases the solubility of toxic metal salts, notably aluminium	High acidity may damage or destroy trout eggs and young trout. Increased concentrations of aluminium salts in the water may also poison all aquatic animal life.
ARTIFICIAL STOCKING	
Lakes and rivers introduction of large or alien trout varieties, often raised artificially	Ousting or hybridization of native wild trout

CAUSE	EFFECT
DAMAGE TO RIVERBED AND BANKS	
Deforestation of river banks	Erosion of banks and silting up of trout redds
Logging, excavation of riverbed	Silt, sand and gravel washed downstream may destroy pools and silt up redds
Canalisation for land drainage	Increased silting, loss of redds, destruction of pools, reduction of water depth
Dam construction	Loss of redds, reduction of flow below the dam, prevention of spawning runs (unless there is a fish-pass). Where the dam is for hydro-electric power generation losses of fish stocks may be caused by pumping cold water into the river
OVERFISHING	
Commercial fisheries Overkill of sea and estuarine trout, and destruction of sea trout foods	Decline in feeding grounds, populations and size of sea trout
Game Anglers Overkill of lake and river trout	Diminishing trout populations. Tendency to introduce alien trout varieties
Poachers Overkill of larger forms of trout, notably sea trout, using nets, poisons and explosives	Decimation of stocks, usually just before spawning, when the trout are most vulnerable

LEFT

LEFT

The River Test, England's famous trout stream, where heavy stocking has resulted in a massive decline of the wild brown trout.

compete with and often displace the native fish. Stocked trout also frequently interbreed with the lake or river's own strain to produce a hybrid trout. But there is evidence that stocked or hybridized trout may have a much lower breeding success than the native wild trout. Consequently, once the native trout have been lost, a large head of trout in the water can be maintained only by continual restocking.

On many of the famous English rivers, like the Hampshire Test and Itchen, the Derbyshire Wye, the Lancashire Ribble and the Yorkshire Aire and Wharfe, anglers now catch lots of large brown trout but very rarely encounter small ones: the young fish up to eight inches in length that would, if the river was generating its natural stock, be the mature fish of one or more years hence. This is almost certainly a consequence of overstocking with very large fish that are not of that river's own native variety.

There are still many rivers and lakes in Europe and North America which have never experienced artificial stocking. Such waters maintain their native stocks of wild trout. It seems imperative that, should angling pressure increase to the point that there are demands for restocking these waters, any artificial stocking should be from the water's own fish. Though this will be more expensive and much slower than the usual system, it will guarantee the genetic integrity of the wild trout population.

Restocking a wild trout lake or river with trout of a different variety or species is perhaps the greatest threat to wild trout. It is always possible to clean up a river and make good the damage caused by damming, canalisation, and deforestation of the river banks. Often a small head of the native trout will have survived either in the feeder streams of lakes or in the highest tributaries of a river, and these will restock the entire water

naturally once the problem in the lake or lower down the river has been solved. But when the wild trout of a river or lake system are destroyed either through failure to compete with larger introduced fish or through hybridization with stock fish, the native variety is gone for ever.

Far better in the long run than haphazard artificial stocking are other solutions that improve the water and conserve its own trout stocks. The first is to ensure that the habitat is brought into pristine condition: that all sources of pollution are removed, that the water is encouraged to produce its maximum supply of trout food, that the gravel redds are kept in good order. The second is to impose bag limits that will ensure the maintenance of a good head of spawning trout. A crucial aspect of bag control, besides restricting the number of fish that an angler may take, is regulating the size of the fish that may be killed. Most fisheries dicatate a minimum size, which means that anglers take the larger trout and return the smaller immature fish. However, by insisting instead that the larger trout should be returned, fisheries can ensure that the older more experienced trout, that will lay more eggs and produce more young, will breed. The third solution, which is also proving very successful in parts of the USA and Europe, is to have parts of river and lake systems declared catch-and-return waters. Besides providing the best angling on the river (because there will be more there to catch), catch-and-return beats will hold a population of trout that can spill over into the beats from which fish are removed.

Also in the USA, some attempts are being made to redress the situation in rivers and lakes where pure stocks of the native trout still exist alongside introduced trout and hybrids. Fishery officers are removing the non-native trout and encouraging the wild trout by artificially propagating them in hatcheries. Anglers are also encouraged to remove as many of the foreigners as possible and to return all native trout. Ed Lusch notes in his book *The Comprehensive Guide to Western Gamefish* (1985) that the Eagle Lake population of rainbow trout 'was once nearly extinct, but the California Department of Fish and Game successfully brought the species back to health again'.

In Britain and Europe, where fishery owners are under great pressure to produce large numbers of big trout, irrespective of their genetic background, this policy has yet to be adopted. Its success will require a great change of attitude by anglers. Most trout fishermen expect not only to catch lots of trout but also to take home a 'bag limit' of four, six or even eight fish per day. For a fishery manager to insist that all indigenous fish must be returned to the water would prove very unpopular. Most anglers also want to catch large trout; usually much larger than the size generated naturally by the river or lake. For a fishery manager to announce that he was no longer stocking with big cultivated trout could amount to financial suicide.

Where, a century ago, European anglers were quite happy to catch wild trout weighing three to the pound, today they are disappointed if they catch any fish less than a pound. The fact that it requires as much angling skill (and possibly more) to catch a $\frac{1}{2}$ lb wild trout as it does to catch a 5 lb trout that has just been released from the stock pen is ignored. The fact that the small wild trout is a perfect and beautiful fish, while the cultivated trout often has malformed fins and lacks the colour of the native fish, is ignored. The fact that the small fish is native and that the big fish has no natural place in the lake or river is ignored. Encouraged by the angling press, so-called angling experts, and the competitive urge to catch more and bigger fish than the next man, the average European trout angler prefers to catch big cultivated trout.

During our research for this book we spoke to many anglers on this subject. One expressed his disappointment at the size of the wild brown trout he had caught during his first visit to some Scottish lochs. Another was quite disgruntled with the size of the cutthroat trout he had caught on his first ("and last") trip to Yellowstone. We hope that this book will help anglers more fully to appreciate the wild trout, and to realise that catching large numbers of big cultivated trout is but one aspect of trout fishing, with its place in waters that have no native trout.

Public concern about 'threatened species' and the risk of 'extinction' is largely focused on a few quite famous, spectacular and well-publicised instances: the white and black rhinos of East Africa, the Californian condor, the blue whale. Endangered varieties or subspecies of organisms that, as species, seem to be widespread and thriving attract very little attention. However, it is as important to protect small natural populations—strains, varieties, sub-species, call them what you will—as it is to conserve whole species. Each variety has just as much genetic integrity as a species; each has evolved over thousands of years. The destruction of any variety means the waste of that time and that evolution. It is the loss of an organism that is unique and can never be replaced.

Slowly this idea is gaining acceptance. In agriculture, for example, many ancient breeds of pigs, sheep, cattle and poultry were ousted earlier this century in favour of modern breeds that met the demand for high productivity. But recently it has been discovered that some of the old varieties had certain merits that the newer ones lack: disease resistance, quality on the table and so on. Now rare breeds establishments have been set up to preserve these ancient varieties. Likewise in horticulture, there

RIGHT

The River Tees, in northeast England, once had prolific runs of Atlantic sea trout. Now gross pollution of the estuary prevents the fish from entering the river. The upper reaches too have been ruined: one accidental spillage of creosote into the river in 1983 destroyed 34 miles of trout stream.

The clean waters of an undamaged estuary. This river holds brown trout and a large run of Atlantic sea trout; bull trout thrive in the estuary, feeding on fish fry and crustaceans. Three varieties in one river, each worthy of conservation.

are field stations where older varieties of pears and apples are being maintained. We believe that the same methods of conservation could and should be applied to wild trout varieties.

The trout of some rivers and lakes are so easily distinguished that they have been given special names; others have not. But the latter are still specialised for life in their own particular lake or river. At present the study of the structure of individual trout populations is in its infancy. But from the first investigations using gel electrophoresis into the genetic structure of local trout populations it seems that it may be possible to say that each river and lake system has its own variety of wild trout. Thus, for the conservation of wild trout, it is not enough that a river has trout in it; the river must have its own trout living in it. Stocking wild trout waters with non-native fish should be a last resort, to be avoided wherever possible.

There are of course situations where waters can only be restocked with non-native varieties. In the industrialised regions of Europe and North America, many lakes and rivers lost their head of fish many years ago; the environmental lobby is encouraging industry and government to clean up such waters. Once these are clean enough to sustain a head of trout, fish must be introduced from a hatchery. Elsewhere, a catastrophic pollution incident may utterly wipe out a population of wild trout. Unless there are already brood fish in captivity, or a sufficient number of survivors in the headwaters or feeder streams, it will be impossible to revive the water's own strain.

Yet these exceptional cases only strengthen the argument, certainly where major river and lake systems are concerned, for maintaining some of the native wild trout in isolation in case of disaster, rather as rare farm animal breeds or plant varieties are preserved. Such a strategy, though expensive, would prove worthwhile if evidence continues to accumulate on the long term damage caused by artificial stocking. The trout farming industry might itself benefit from such a system. A great deal of research is being carried out today into genetic engineering in trout stocks destined for the fishmonger or put-and-take trout fisheries. It may be discovered that genes special to wild trout confer resistance to disease or parasites; or affect growth rate or other physiological or behavioural traits. This would make the conservation of wild trout varieties doubly important.

Over the last century or more, numerous varieties of trout have been lost for ever, while others remain in danger of extinction. Today we are learning from our mistakes, if only very slowly. Increasingly the environmental lobby is being listened to by those planners who seek to exploit our lakes and rivers. It is essential that this process continues. Only if those bodies responsible for rivers, lakes, estuaries and seas, the owners and controllers of fisheries, anglers and conservationists all act together will future generations have clean, productive waters; and wild trout living in them.

THE PYRAMID LAKE TROUT

Of all American wild trout, few have suffered a worse decline than the wild trout of Pyramid Lake. Set in the desert regions of western Nevada, Pyramid Lake is one of a series of lakes, including Walker Lake on the Walker River, Cascade, Fallen Leaf and Summit Lakes, and Lake Tahoe on the California-Nevada border, that hold or used to hold stocks of the cutthroat subspecies *Salmo clarki henshawi*.

In Ice Age times, all of these lakes together with their river systems were part of a massive lake called Lake Lahontan: hence the name Lahontan cutthroat is given to the form of trout native to this region. It has been estimated that, at its maximum size some 25,000 years ago, Lake Lahontan covered about 8500 square miles with depths of up to 875 feet. As the climate warmed the lake shrank to leave the present smaller remnants and feeder streams surrounded by desert.

Some authorities consider that the cutthroats inhabiting the streams that drain into the eastern side of the ancient Lake Lahontan basin constitute a separate variety (the subspecies name *Salmo clarki humboltensis* has been suggested for these); but the differences between the varieties are fairly trivial.

Until the early years of this century, the Pyramid Lake cutthroats were famous for their size. The record is for a 41lb fish taken from the lake by John Skimmerhorn in July 1925; and some evidence exists that Indians and commercial netsmen formerly caught much bigger fish, possibly as large as 60lbs. In the last natural spawning run of the original Pyramid Lake stock, in 1938, the average size of trout was reported as 20lbs.

Apart from Lake Tahoe, none of the other lakes of the Lahontan basin ever produced fish of such size. This has been explained by the fact that Pyramid Lake trout are piscivorous, and had an abundant fish-food source in the form of tui chub; at the same time they had the genetic constitution that enabled them to grow to large size. Other lakes, with the Lahontan cutthroat but without tui chub, have been stocked with small fish; the trout have fed on them but never attained the size of the original Pyramid Lake trout.

The stocks of large trout attracted commercial netsmen. Between October 1888 and April 1889 almost 100 tons of Lahontan trout were taken from the Pyramid and Tahoe Lake systems and shipped for export. It is not clear just how badly this exploitation damaged the native trout of Pyramid Lake; but overfishing certainly caused the demise of the Tahoe and Walker Lake stocks. However, the Pyramid Lake trout were doomed later by the construction of the Derby Dam on the Truckee River: a major feeder stream of Pyramid Lake and the main spawning stream for the Pyramid Lake cutthroat.

The dam was completed in 1905. It diverted most of the Truckee River flow to the Carson River, with the consequence that the Truckee virtually dried up: the last spawning run was in 1938. The shallow Lake Winnemucca, that shared the Truckee River with Pyramid Lake, soon disappeared. And the level of Pyramid Lake fell by 70 feet in 50 years.

The cutthroats of the other Lahontan lakes and river systems disappeared when the waters were artificially stocked with other forms of trout, notably rainbow. The wild varieties were lost either through failure to compete

Pyramid Lake is set amidst the desert landscape of Nevada. The map also shows the outline of Winnemucca Lake, now dried up, to the east of Pyramid.

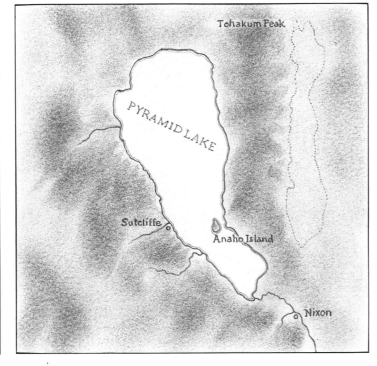

with the foreign trout, or through interbreeding.

Though the pure Lahontan cutthroat was once thought extinct, remnant populations have been discovered. These have been propagated articially and are being used to restock waters that held this variety of trout, after the non-native fish have been removed. However, Pyramid Lake and Lake Tahoe are unlikely ever to produce trout of the size they once did; and they will never again produce spawning runs where the trout average 20 lbs.

THE GREENBACK TROUT

The greenback cutthroat *Salmo clarki stomias* is a variety native to the Arkansas and South Platte river drainage basins of Colorado. When the first white settlers arrived in this region the greenback was apparently abundant. However, water abstraction and diversion of streams for irrigation, pollution from mining spoil, and overfishing decimated the stocks. Then the European brown trout and the American speckled char were introduced, followed by rainbow trout and other forms of cutthroat. These ousted many of the native greenbacks by competition, and interbred with the remaining population producing hybrid stocks.

In *Cutthroat*, Patrick Trotter records that, though the strain was considered extinct by 1937, thorough surveys made in the 1960s discovered two relict pure greenback populations: one in a tributary of North Boulder Creek and the other in the headwaters of South Poudre River.

Elsewhere, hybrid cutthroat stocks still exhibit some of the characteristics of the greenback.

This variety of cutthroat is on the lists of endangered species of the 1973 US Endangered Species Act and the State of Colorado list of 1976. Big efforts are being made to rear pure greenbacks in captivity and then release them into their former range; and at the same time to remove the non-native trout. As a result, the survival of one form of wild trout, that was on the verge of extinction, at last seems assured.

ABOVE

A greenback cutthroat. Once thought extinct, the greenback is now being nurtured to recovery.

Pencil and wash

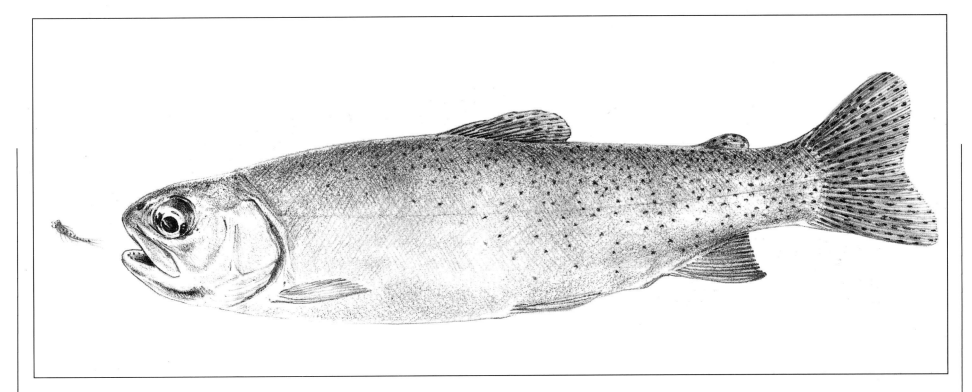

THE YELLOWFIN TROUT

The story of the yellowfin cutthroat, initially named *Salmo mykiss macdonaldi* in 1891 after the US Fish Commissioner MacDonald, (now *Salmo clarki macdonaldi*) is one of the most mysterious of all wild trout stories. The variety appeared as if from nowhere; and has now disappeared without trace.

At the retreat of the last glaciation, boulder clay morraine blocked off a tributary of the headwaters of the Arkansas River in what is now the state of Colorado. Two lakes were formed, which the early settlers named Twin Lakes. They were known to hold small greenback cutthroat from the early days of the Wild West, but in the mid-1880s there were reports of much larger trout, up to 10 lb in weight, with bright yellow fins.

In July 1889, Professor D. S. Jordan and G. R. Fisher visited Twin Lakes, and published their discoveries in the 1891 *Bulletin of the US Fish Commission*. They found both the greenback and the new yellowfin cutthroat. In his report Jordan named the latter and described it as follows: 'Color, silvery olive; a broad lemon yellow shade along the sides, lower fins bright golden yellow in life, no red anywhere except the deep red dash on each side of the throat'.

Jordan's specimens were recently re-examined by the American biologists Robert Behnke, who concluded that, 'I have no doubt that Jordan was correct; the yellowfin trout and the greenback trout from Twin Lakes were two distinct groups of cutthroat trout.'

Through to about 1903, greenback and yellowfin cutthroats survived together in Twin Lakes, remaining isolated as both breeders and feeders. Then the introduced rainbow trout took a firm hold; the greenback population was ruined by hybridization and the yellowfin completely disappeared. The introduction of a foreign trout had resulted in the loss of a special form of wild trout: for ever.

THE GOLDEN TROUT

These quite special trout varieties of the southwest of the USA and Mexico are possibly America's oldest varieties in evolutionary terms. With one exception, they have all been brought close to extinction as pure, true-breeding forms. That exception is the South Fork Kern River Golden Trout, which is raised in fish farms and used to stock mountain streams throughout the west of the USA. The others have suffered greatly due to the introduction of non-native trout varieties that have either ousted these little trout from their home streams or interbred with them so that the true variety has become very rare.

Pure Apache and Gila trout populations are extremely scarce. The Gilbert Golden trout exists in its original state only on small streams above natural barriers which the introduced trout cannot pass. Pure Mexican trout occur only in the highest tributaries of their native rivers. Attempts are being made to exterminate the introduced trout from some of the streams within the traditional ranges of these wild trout varieties, and to increase the stocks of wild trout.

Most of these trout inhabit high level streams, at altitudes up to 10,000 feet above sea level. In summer the nights are very cold, though the temperature during the day might reach 30° Centigrade. And the winters are long: the growing season may last for only four or five months. Over much of the countryside, huge pine stands dominate alpine meadows of lush tall grass. On exposed rocky bluffs the plant cover consists of short, squat alpines that grow slowly through the short summer and are then hidden away through the long winters.

These uplands are drained by feeder streams and headwaters that join to make large rivers in the lower valleys and on the coastal plain. Upstream, the water is cold and well-oxygenated; but it produces only small amounts of aquatic trout foods. In fact, much of the food taken by the high level trout originates from the surrounding countryside: flies, beetles, moths and other insects that are blown on to the water. Since many of the streams and lakes at these altitudes are iced up from October to June, the trout must feed, grow and breed in the short summer.

Their growth rate is very slow. At ten inches, a Gilbert or South Fork Kern River golden trout is a large fish, as is an eight inch Gila, Apache or Mexican golden trout. These varieties might grow much larger were the water more productive: one South Fork Kern River golden trout introduced into Cooks Lake, Wyoming weighed 11lbs 4oz when caught. Similarly an Apache trout caught in Bear Canyon Lake, Arizona scaled 3lbs 10oz.

The taxonomic status of these trout has been the subject of much controversy. Many of their distinct characteristics, for instance colour, are altered when the fish are taken from their native waters and introduced into lowland streams and lakes. Golden trout, for example, become much darker and duller in colour. This suggests that their characteristic coloration is controlled at least in part by the environment, possibly as a protective camouflage.

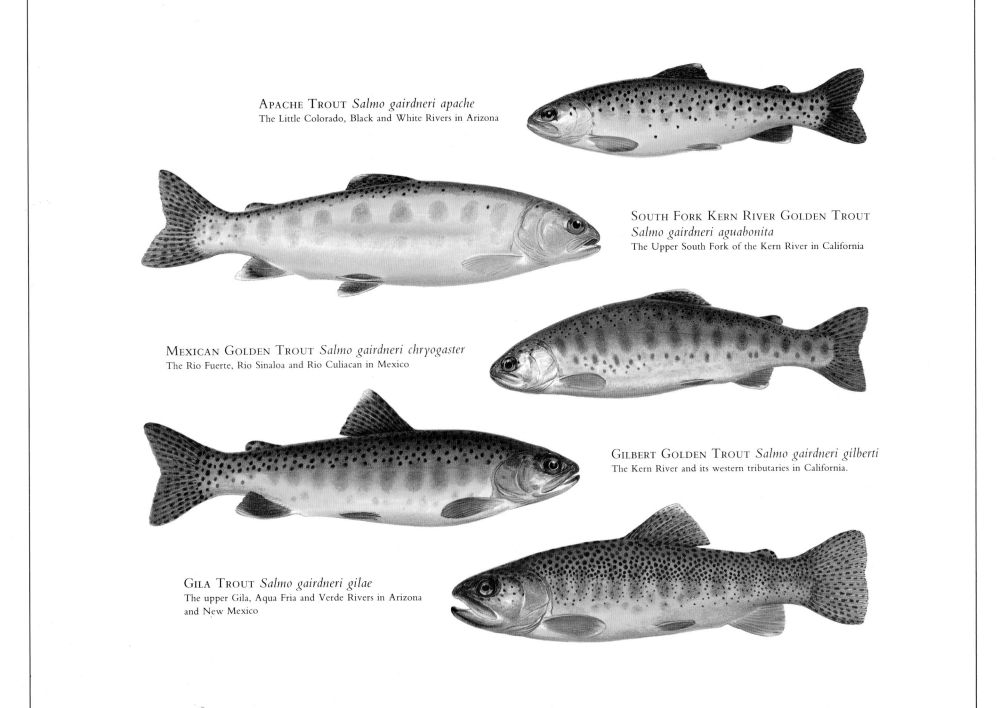

APACHE TROUT *Salmo gairdneri apache*
The Little Colorado, Black and White Rivers in Arizona

SOUTH FORK KERN RIVER GOLDEN TROUT
Salmo gairdneri aguabonita
The Upper South Fork of the Kern River in California

MEXICAN GOLDEN TROUT *Salmo gairdneri chryogaster*
The Rio Fuerte, Rio Sinaloa and Rio Culiacan in Mexico

GILBERT GOLDEN TROUT *Salmo gairdneri gilberti*
The Kern River and its western tributaries in California.

GILA TROUT *Salmo gairdneri gilae*
The upper Gila, Aqua Fria and Verde Rivers in Arizona
and New Mexico

GLOSSARY

Life History

Redd A shallow trench cut in the riverbed by the hen trout, in which the eggs are laid and fertilized. The term is sometimes also used to describe the banks of gravel where the trout spawn.

Milt A milky fluid produced by the testes of the cock trout that contains the sperm.

Ova The hen trout's eggs, which are laid in a redd and then fertilized by the milt. The same term is used for embryo trout while they are developing within the egg membrane. Thus ova can be described as 'un-eyed', where the embryo has not developed eyes, or 'eyed' where the embryo eyes are clearly visible beneath the egg membrane.

Alevin The young trout after it has left the egg. It retains the large yolk sac from which it obtains its food supplies, and remains hidden in the gravel surrounding the redd. In North America alevins are sometimes called 'sac-fry'.

Fry The young trout after it has exhausted the yolk supplies and begun to seek food. Sometimes the fry stage is split into two: *unfed fry* where the fry has not begun to feed, but has lost the alevin yolk sac; *fed fry* where the fry is feeding actively.

Parr The older fry stage, where ovoid 'parr markings' are well developed along the side of the fish.

THE ANATOMY OF THE TROUT

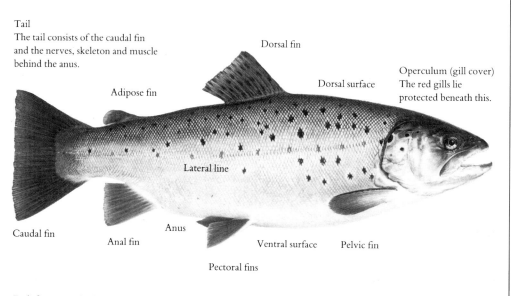

Tail
The tail consists of the caudal fin and the nerves, skeleton and muscle behind the anus.

Dorsal fin

Dorsal surface

Operculum (gill cover)
The red gills lie protected beneath this.

Adipose fin

Lateral line

Caudal fin

Anus

Anal fin

Ventral surface

Pelvic fin

Pectoral fins

Each fin except the fatty adipose fin consists of a series of skeletal rays, with muscle tissue between them so that they can be used for manoeuvering.

In trout the dorsal surface is always darker than the ventral surface: a camouflage adaptation.

The front lower jaw develops as a hooked extension in cock fish during the breeding season. The kype is usually less hooked in trout than in salmon.

Smolt The post-parr form in which the young of sea-going trout migrate from freshwater to the sea.

Post-smolt A term sometimes used to describe the period of the life of the sea trout between its arrival in the sea and its return to freshwater as a sexually mature fish. This term might also include those steelhead, cutthroat and Atlantic sea trout that return to freshwater after a few months at sea but which do not breed (*herling*); these later return to the sea before returning as adult sea trout.

Kelt The adult trout after spawning; the rigours of the breeding season result in a massive wastage of body tissues so that the condition of kelts is usually poor. Recovering kelts are sometimes called 'mended' or 'well-mended kelts'. Those that recover completely can be difficult to separate from 'maiden' trout (those that have yet to spawn) other than by scale reading.

Scale reading A technique whereby the life history of an individual trout can be deduced from the microscopic examination of its scales. As the trout grows it lays down rings, analogous to the annual rings laid down by trees, on each scale. From these can be ascertained the age of the fish, in sea trout the number of years of river and sea life, and whether the fish has bred.

Genetics and Evolution

Genes Chemical molecules, held within the nucleus of the cells that make up the body of the trout, which determine growth, form and structure, coloration, physiology and behaviour of the trout. An individual obtains half of its genes from each parent. Variation in genetic structure can result in one individual or one population of trout being quite distinct from other individuals or populations.

The effect of genes within an individual or population can be greatly modified by environmental factors, so there may be argument as to whether a physical feature in the trout really is a consequence of genes.

Gel electrophoresis A modern chemical technique (also known as 'genetic fingerprinting') that can determine precisely the genetic composition of a population of trout. Gel elecrophoresis has proved that some trout populations and varieties are genetically discrete, and not the result of environmental factors.

Evolution The process whereby the genetic structure of a trout population is moulded by the environment. The pressures of natural selection will tend to remove some genes in favour of other advantageous genes that render the trout population better adapted to its environment. Thus two lakes or rivers, colonised by trout from one population, may give rise to two genetically different trout populations.

Taxonomic status The differences between populations of trout may be such that the populations can be named as separate *species*, or *subspecies* within one species, or *varieties* within one subspecies of a species. Which of these three categories a population of trout is placed in depends largely on the arbitrary opinion of taxonomic biologists, as the rules that define the terms species, subspecies and variety have many exceptions.

Aquatic Environment

Oligotrophic The purest of waters that produce little trout food and where trout populations are small and growth rate slow.

Eutrophic Lakes and rivers that produce large amounts of animal and plant life. Such waters may have large populations of fast-growing trout.

Mesotrophic Waters that lie between the extremes of oligotrophic and eutrophic conditions. Because eutrophic waters may verge on the state of over-eutrophication, mesotrophic waters are perhaps the ideal trout habitats.

Over-eutrophication Waters that have artificial fertilisers or organic pollutants added may frequently suffer from oxygen shortage, especially in spells of hot dry weather. This usually results in a death of trout.

Pollution The addition of material to water that results in an alteration to the plant and animal communities of that water. Pollutants may be e.g. *organic* (raw sewage, wood pulp) or *inorganic* (chemical fertilizers, disolved gases from 'acid rain', lead from mining, cyanide from industrial outfalls).

BIBLIOGRAPHY

AELIANUS, Claudius (n.d.) *De Animalium Natura*

BEHNKE, Robert J. (1979) *Monograph of the Native Trouts of the Genus* Salmo *of Western North America*

BERNERS, Dame Juliana (1496) *Treetyse of Fysshynge wyth an Angle*

BLACKER, W. (1842) *The Art of Angling*

BLAKEY, Robert (1800) *Angling*

DARWIN, Charles (1859) *On the Origin of Species*

FAHY, Edward (1985) *Child of the Tides*

FALKUS, Hugh (1962) *Sea Trout Fishing*

FALLODEN, Viscount Grey (1899) *Fly-Fishing*

FERGUSON, Andrew (1985) *Went Memorial Lecture* (Royal Dublin Society)

FERGUSON, Andrew & MASON, F.M. (1981) *Journal of Fish Biology*

FROST, W.E. & BROWN M.E. (1967) *The Trout*

GREENHALGH, Malcolm (1987) *Trout Fishing in Rivers*

GREENHALGH, Malcolm (1987) *Lake, Loch and Reservoir Trout Fishing*

GÜNTER, A. (1880) *Introduction to the Study of Fishes*

HOUGHTON, W. (1879) *British Freshwater Fishes*

JOHNSON, Les (1971) *Fishing the Sea-Run Cutthroat Trout*

JOHNSON, Les (1979) *Sea-Run*

JORDAN, D.S. & EVERMANN, B.W. (1896–1898) *The Fishes of North and Middle America*

LUCH, Bill (1976) *Steelhead Drift Fishing*

LUSCH, Ed (1985) *The Comprehensive Guide to Western Gamefish*

MOORE, T.C. Kingsmill (1960) *A Man may Fish*

OLIVER, Stephen (1832) *Scenes and Recollections of Fly-Fishing*

PALAEOECOLOGY RESEARCH UNIT (1988) *Lake Acidification in the United Kingdom*

PENNELL, H.C. (1885) *Fishing: Salmon and Trout*

RAYMOND, Steve (2nd Ed. 1980) *Kamloops*

REGAN C. Tate (1911) *The Freshwater Fishes of the British Isles*

SALMON, TROUT & SEA TROUT MAGAZINE (UK) September 1988

SCHWEIBERT, Ernest (1979) *Trout*

SMITH, Robert H. (1984) *Native Trout of North America*

SKUES, G.E.M. (1910) *Minor Tactics of the Chalk Stream*

TROTTER, Patrick C. (1987) *Cutthroat: Native Trout of the West*

VINES, Sydney (1984) *Frank Sawyer: Man of the Riverside*

WALTON, Izaak (5th Ed. 1676) *The Compleat Angler*

WHEELER, A. (1969) *The Fishes of the British Isles and Europe*

YARRELL, William (3rd Ed. 1859) *A History of British Fishes*

Index

PICTURE CREDITS

The paintings, drawings and maps reproduced in this book are
all by Rod Sutterby, with the exception of the angler's map
of Loch Leven (p.29), which was supplied by James Philip,
Kinross.

The photographs are all by Simon Farrell, with the exception
of Yellowstone Lake (p.25), Yellowstone River (p.54), Snake
River (p.59) and Crescent Lake (p.82) by The Image Bank;
Kamloops Lake (p.89) by Spectrum Colour Library;
Yellowstone Lake (p.94) by Frank Lane Picture Agency;
Columbia River (p.108), Columbia River (p.116) by The
Image Bank; Logging on Kamloops River (p.118) by
Spectrum Colour Library; and Agricultural pollution,
Cambridgeshire (p.119) by Peter Ward.